Contents

What do you think of this book? We want to hear from you!

Microsoft is interested in hearing your feedback so we can continually improve our books and learning resources for you. To participate in a brief online survey, please visit:

www.microsoft.com/learning/booksurvey/

Microsoft®

Expression® Design

Sara Froehlich
Marc Campbell

PUBLISHED BY
Microsoft Press
A Division of Microsoft Corporation
One Microsoft Way
Redmond, Washington 98052-6399

Library of Congress Control Number: X14-25711

Printed and bound in the United States of America.

1 2 3 4 5 6 7 8 9   QWT   3 2 1 0 9 8

Distributed in Canada by H.B. Fenn and Company Ltd.

A CIP catalogue record for this book is available from the British Library.

Microsoft Press books are available through booksellers and distributors worldwide. For further information about international editions, contact your local Microsoft Corporation office or contact Microsoft Press International directly at fax (425) 936-7329. Visit our Web site at www.microsoft.com/mspress. Send comments to mspinput@microsoft.com.

Microsoft, Microsoft Press, Aero, Expression, Expression Blend, Internet Explorer, SharePoint, Silverlight, Windows, Windows Media, Windows Server, and Windows Vista are either registered trademarks or trademarks of Microsoft Corporation in the United States and/or other countries. Other product and company names mentioned herein may be the trademarks of their respective owners.

The example companies, organizations, products, domain names, e-mail addresses, logos, people, places, and events depicted herein are fictitious. No association with any real company, organization, product, domain name, e-mail address, logo, person, place, or event is intended or should be inferred.

This book expresses the author's views and opinions. The information contained in this book is provided without any express, statutory, or implied warranties. Neither the authors, Microsoft Corporation, nor its resellers, or distributors will be held liable for any damages caused or alleged to be caused either directly or indirectly by this book.

Acquisitions Editor: Juliana Aldous Atkinson
Developmental Editor: Sandra Haynes
Project Editor: Rosemary Caperton
Editorial Production: Online Training Solutions, Inc.
Technical Reviewers: Mark Dodge and Paul Jackson; Technical Review services provided by Content Master, a member of CM Group, Ltd.

Body Part No. X14-25711

Your All-in-One Resource

On the CD that accompanies this book, you'll find additional resources to extend your learning.

The reference library includes the following fully searchable titles:

- *Microsoft Computer Dictionary*, 5th ed.
- Windows Vista Product Guide

The CD interface has a new look. You can use the tabs for an assortment of tasks:

- Check for book updates (if you have Internet access)
- Install the book's practice files
- Go online for product support or CD support
- Send us feedback

The following screen shot gives you a glimpse of the new interface.

6 Using Fills   125

7 Using Strokes   149

8 Working with Text   171

9 Working with Bitmap Images   199

What do you think of this book? We want to hear from you!

Microsoft is interested in hearing your feedback so we can continually improve our books and learning resources for you. To participate in a brief online survey, please visit:

www.microsoft.com/learning/booksurvey/

Introducing Expression Design

Microsoft Expression Design is a professional design tool used to create vector and bitmap illustrations and elements for desktop publishing, print, and the Web. Traditional shape tools and drawing tools—such as the Pen, Polyline, and B-Spline tools—give the artist or illustrator everything necessary for dramatic and creative illustrations. By using skeletal strokes to provide the utmost in editing power, brush strokes are placed along vector paths, keeping the strokes fully editable, even one anchor point at a time, for total control and precision. Brush strokes can emulate artistic media like watercolors and acrylics for unique capabilities in a vector illustration program.

Expression Design is part of Microsoft Expression Studio, which is an integrated group of applications that, in addition to Expression Design, includes the following:

- **Expression Blend.** A professional design tool used to create engaging, Web-connected multimedia experiences for Windows.
- **Expression Web.** A professional design tool used to create modern, standards-based sites that deliver superior quality on the Web.
- **Expression Media.** A professional asset management tool for visually cataloging and organizing all your digital assets, and that provides for effortless retrieval and presentation.

Today's graphic designers work in a variety of media, and the ability to use one suite of integrated products to provide clients with designs for print, the Web, and animation is a great time saver. Microsoft Expression Studio provides the tools and the power to work for all types of output in one package.

Information for Readers Running Windows XP

The graphics and operating system–related instructions in this book reflect the Windows Vista user interface. However, Windows Vista is not required; you can also use a computer running Windows XP with Service Pack 2 (SP2) installed.

Most of the differences you will encounter when working through the exercises in this book on a computer running Windows XP relate to appearance rather than functionality. For example, the Windows Vista Start button is round rather than rectangular and is not labeled with the word *Start*; window frames and window-management buttons look different; and if your system supports Windows Aero, the window frames might be transparent.

In this section, we provide steps for navigating to or through menus and dialog boxes in Windows XP that differ from those provided in the exercises in this book. For the most part, these differences are small enough that you will have no difficulty in completing the exercises.

Managing the Practice Files

The instructions given in the "Using the Book's CD" section are specific to Windows Vista. The only differences when installing, using, uninstalling, and removing the practice files supplied on the companion CD are the default installation location and the uninstall process.

On a computer running Windows Vista, the default installation location of the practice files is *Documents\Microsoft Press\Expression Design SBS*. On a computer running Windows XP, the default installation location is *My Documents\Microsoft Press\Expression Design SBS*. If your computer is running Windows XP, whenever an exercise tells you to navigate to your *Documents* folder, you should instead go to your *My Documents* folder.

To uninstall the practice files from a computer running Windows XP:

1. On the Windows taskbar, click the **Start** button, and then click **Control Panel**.
2. In **Control Panel**, click (or in Classic view, double-click) **Add or Remove Programs**.
3. In the **Add or Remove Programs** window, click **Microsoft Expression Design Step by Step**, and then click **Remove**.
4. In the **Add or Remove Programs** message box asking you to confirm the deletion, click **Yes**.

Using the Start Menu

Folders on the Windows Vista Start menu expand vertically. Folders on the Windows XP Start menu expand horizontally. However, the steps to access a command on the Start menu are identical on both systems.

To start Microsoft Expression Design on a computer running Windows XP:

→ Click the **Start** button, point to **All Programs**, click **Microsoft Expression**, and then click **Microsoft Expression Design**.

Navigating Dialog Boxes

On a computer running Windows XP, some of the dialog boxes you will work with in the exercises not only look different from the graphics shown in this book but also work differently. These dialog boxes are primarily those that act as an interface between Expression Design and the operating system, including any dialog box in which you navigate to a specific location.

For example, to navigate to the *My Pictures* folder in Windows XP:

→ On the **Start menu**, click **My Pictures**.

To move back to the *My Documents* folder in Windows XP:

Up One Level

→ On the toolbar, click the **Up One Level** button.

Features and Conventions of This Book

This book has been designed to lead you step by step through all the tasks you are most likely to want to perform in Microsoft Expression Design. If you start at the beginning and work your way through all the exercises, you will gain enough proficiency to be able to create complex illustrations by using vector and bitmap tools. However, each topic is also self contained. If you have worked with another graphic design program, or if you completed all the exercises and later need help remembering how to perform a procedure, the following features of this book will help you locate specific information:

- **Detailed table of contents.** Scan this listing of the topics and sidebars within each chapter to quickly find the information you want.
- **Chapter thumb tabs.** Easily locate the beginning of the chapter you want.
- **Topic-specific running heads.** Within a chapter, quickly locate the topic you want by looking at the running head of odd-numbered pages.
- **Detailed index.** Look up specific tasks and features and general concepts in the index, which has been carefully crafted with the reader in mind.
- **Companion CD.** Install the practice files needed for the step-by-step exercises, and consult a fully searchable electronic version of this book and other useful resources contained on this CD.

In addition, we provide a glossary of terms for those times when you need to look up the meaning of a word or the definition of a concept.

You can save time when you use this book by understanding how the *Step by Step* series shows special instructions, keys to press, buttons to click, and so on.

Convention	Meaning
	This icon indicates a reference to the book's companion CD.
USE	This paragraph preceding a step-by-step exercise indicates the practice files or programs that you will use when working through the exercise.
BE SURE TO	This paragraph preceding or following a step-by-step exercise indicates any requirements you should attend to before beginning the exercise or actions you should take to restore your system after completing the exercise.
OPEN	This paragraph preceding a step-by-step exercise indicates files that you should open before beginning the exercise.
CLOSE	Large numbered steps guide you through hands-on exercises in each topic.
1 **2**	Large numbered steps guide you through hands-on exercises in each topic.
1 2	Small numbered steps guide you through procedures in sidebars and in expository text.
→	An arrow indicates a procedure that has only one step.
Tip	These paragraphs give you a helpful hint or shortcut that makes working through a task easier, or information about other available options.
Important	These paragraphs point out information that you need to know to complete a procedure.
Troubleshooting	These paragraphs warn you of potential missteps that might prevent you from continuing with the exercise.
See Also	These paragraphs direct you to more information about a given topic in this book or elsewhere.
Enter	In step-by-step exercises, keys you must press appear as they would on a keyboard.
Ctrl + Tab	A plus sign (+) between two key names means that you must hold down the first key while you press the second key. For example, "Press Ctrl + Tab " means "hold down the Ctrl key while you press the Tab key."
Program interface elements and **user input**	In steps, the names of program elements (such as buttons, commands, and dialog boxes) and text that you are supposed to type are shown in bold characters.
Glossary terms	Terms explained in the glossary are shown in bold italic characters.
Paths and emphasized words	Folder paths, URLs, and emphasized words are shown in italic characters.

Using the Book's CD

The CD inside the back cover of this book contains the practice files you'll use as you work through the exercises in this book. By using practice files, you can jump right in and concentrate on learning how to get the most of out of Microsoft Expression Design.

CD Contents

The following table lists the practice files necessary to complete the exercises.

Chapter	Practice files
Chapter 1: Working with Documents	*WorkingDocuments\pear.design* *WorkingDocuments\tree.design*
Chapter 2: Navigating the Workspace	*NavigatingWorkspace\pear.design* *NavigatingWorkspace\tree.design*
Chapter 3: Manipulating Objects	*ManipulatingObjects\hearts.design* *ManipulatingObjects\objects.design*
Chapter 4: Working with Layers	*UnderstandingLayers\layers.design*
Chapter 5: Using the Drawing Tools	*UsingDrawingTools\B-Spline1.design* *UsingDrawingTools\B-Spline2.design* *UsingDrawingTools\clipping_paths.design* *UsingDrawingTools\compound_paths.design* *UsingDrawingTools\path_operations.design* *UsingDrawingTools\pentool.design* *UsingDrawingTools\polyline1.design* *UsingDrawingTools\polyline2.design*
Chapter 6: Using Fills	*UsingFills\heart.design* *UsingFills\my_rose.design* *UsingFills\paintbrush.design* *UsingFills\pattern.bmp* *UsingFills\properties_panel.design*

continued

Chapter	Practice files
Chapter 7: Using Strokes	*UsingStrokes\blends.design* *UsingStrokes\hand.design* *UsingStrokes\my_heart.design* *UsingStrokes\paths_and_clones.design* *UsingStrokes\redrose.png* *UsingStrokes\save_stroke.design*
Chapter 8: Working with Text	*WorkingText\abc.design* *WorkingText\barchart.design* *WorkingText\ransom.design* *WorkingText\smile.design* *WorkingText\smile_dot.design* *WorkingText\valentine.design* *WorkingText\wordballoon.design*
Chapter 9: Working with Bitmap Images	*WorkingBitmaps\berries.bmp* *WorkingBitmaps\ghost.design* *WorkingBitmaps\leaves.bmp* *WorkingBitmaps\pumpkin.design* *WorkingBitmaps\trickortreat.design*
Chapter 10: Exporting and Printing Your Work	*ExportingWork\dragon.design* *ExportingWork\keyboard.design* *ExportingWork\knight.design* *ExportingWork\lamp_squirrel.design* *ExportingWork\phrenology.design* *ExportingWork\water.design*

In addition to the practice files, the CD also includes exciting resources that will enhance your ability to get the most out of using this book and Expression Design, including an electronic version of the book in PDF format.

Minimum System Requirements

To use this book, your computer should meet the following requirements:

- **Processor.** Pentium 700 megahertz (MHz) or higher; 2 gigahertz (GHz) recommended.
- **Memory.** 512 megabytes (MB) of RAM; 1 gigabyte (GB) or more recommended.

- **Hard disk.** For the eBooks and downloads, we recommend 3 GB of available hard disk space with 2 GB on the hard disk where the operating system is installed.

- **Operating system.** Windows Vista or later, Windows XP with Service Pack 2 (SP2), or Windows Server 2003 with Service Pack 1 (SP1) or later.

- **Drive.** CD or DVD drive.

- **Display.** Monitor with 1024x768 or higher screen resolution and 16-bit or higher color depth.

- **Software.** Microsoft Expression Design.

> **Tip** Actual requirements and product functionality may vary based on your system configuration and operating system.

Installing the Practice Files

You must install the practice files on your hard disk before you can use them in the chapters' exercises. Follow these steps to prepare the CD's files for your use.

> **Important** Installing the practice files requires the privileges of a local system administrator.

To install the files from the CD:

1. Remove the companion CD from the envelope at the back of the book, and insert it into the CD drive of your computer.

   The Step By Step Companion CD License Terms appear. Follow the on-screen directions. To use the practice files, you must accept the terms of the license agreement. After you accept the license agreement, a menu screen appears.

   > **Important** If the menu screen does not appear, click the Start button and then click Computer. Display the Folders list in the Navigation Pane, click the icon for your CD drive, and then in the right pane, double-click the StartCD.exe file.

2. Click **Install Practice Files**.

   If you are installing the practice files on a computer running Windows Vista, a File Download – Security Warning dialog box opens.

3. Click **Run**, and when an **Internet Explorer – Security** dialog box opens, click **Run**. The Microsoft Expression Design Step By Step dialog box opens.

4. Click **Next** on the first screen, click **I accept the terms in the license agreement**, and then click **Next**.

5. If you want to install the practice files to a location other than the default folder (*Documents\Microsoft Press\Expression Design SBS*), click the **Change** button, select the new drive and path, and then click **OK**.

> **Important** If you install the practice files to a location other than the default, you will need to substitute that path within the exercises.

6. Click **Next** on the **Choose Destination Location** screen, and then click **Install** on the **Ready to Install the Program** screen to install the selected practice files. If a User Account dialog box opens stating that an unidentified program wants to access your computer, click **Allow**.

7. After the practice files have been installed, click **Finish**.

8. Close the **Step by Step Companion CD** window, remove the companion CD from the CD drive, and return it to the envelope at the back of the book.

Using the Practice Files

When you install the practice files from the companion CD, the files are stored on your hard disk in chapter-specific subfolders under *Documents\Microsoft Press\Expression Design SBS*.

Wherever possible, each chapter is started with the default settings in Expression Design. To reset the workspace, click Reset Active Workspace on the Window menu. Then type D to set the stroke and fill to the default settings. Although you do not have to complete every chapter in order, some exercises make use of user-created files.

A Housekeeping segment at the beginning of each chapter explains any preparation you need to take before you start working through the chapter, as shown here:

> **Important** Before you can use the practice files in this chapter, you need to install them from the book's companion CD to their default location. See "Installing the Practice Files."

Each exercise within a chapter is preceded by a Housekeeping segment that lists the practice files needed for that exercise. The text also explains any preparation you need to take before you start working through the exercise, as shown here:

USE the *tree.design* file. This practice file is located in the *Documents\Microsoft Press\ Expression Design SBS\WorkingDocuments* folder.

BE SURE TO start Expression Design before beginning this exercise.

OPEN the *tree.design* file.

You can browse to the practice files in Windows Explorer by following these steps:

Start

1. On the Windows taskbar, click the **Start** button, and then click **Documents**.

2. In your *Documents* folder, double-click *Microsoft Press*, double-click *Expression Design SBS*, and then double-click a specific chapter folder. The folders are named to correspond to their respective chapters.

Removing the Practice Files

You can free up hard disk space by uninstalling the practice files that were installed from the companion CD. The uninstall process deletes any files that you created in the *Documents\Microsoft Press\Expression Design SBS* folder while working through the exercises.

Follow these steps:

Start

1. On the Windows taskbar, click the **Start** button, and then click **Control Panel**.

2. Under **Programs**, click **Uninstall a program**.

3. Click **Microsoft Office Expression Design Step by Step**, and then click **Uninstall**.

4. In the **Programs And Features** dialog box, click **Yes**.

5. In the **User Account Control** dialog box, click **Allow**.

Important Microsoft Product Support Services does not provide support for this book or its companion CD.

Getting Help

Every effort has been made to ensure the accuracy of this book and the contents of its CD. If you run into problems, please contact the appropriate source, listed in the following sections, for assistance.

Getting Help with This Book and Its CD

If your question or issue concerns the content of this book or its companion CD, please first search the online Microsoft Press Knowledge Base, which provides support information for known errors in or corrections to this book, at the following Web site:

www.microsoft.com/mspress/support/search.asp

If you do not find your answer in the online Knowledge Base, send your comments or questions to Microsoft Learning Technical Support at:

mspinput@microsoft.com

Getting Help with Microsoft Expression Design

If your question is about Microsoft Expression Design, and not about the content of this Microsoft Press book, help is available from the Help menu of Expression Design itself. Click Help, and then click User Guide or press F1.

If you need additional help, please search the Microsoft Help and Support Center or the Microsoft Knowledge Base at:

support.microsoft.com

In the United States, Microsoft software product support issues not covered by the Microsoft Knowledge Base are addressed by Microsoft Product Support Services. The Microsoft software support options available from Microsoft Product Support Services are listed at:

www.microsoft.com/services/microsoftservices/srv_support.mspx

Outside the United States, for support information specific to your location, please refer to the Worldwide Support menu on the Microsoft Help And Support Web site for the site specific to your country:

support.microsoft.com/common/international.aspx

Chapter at a Glance

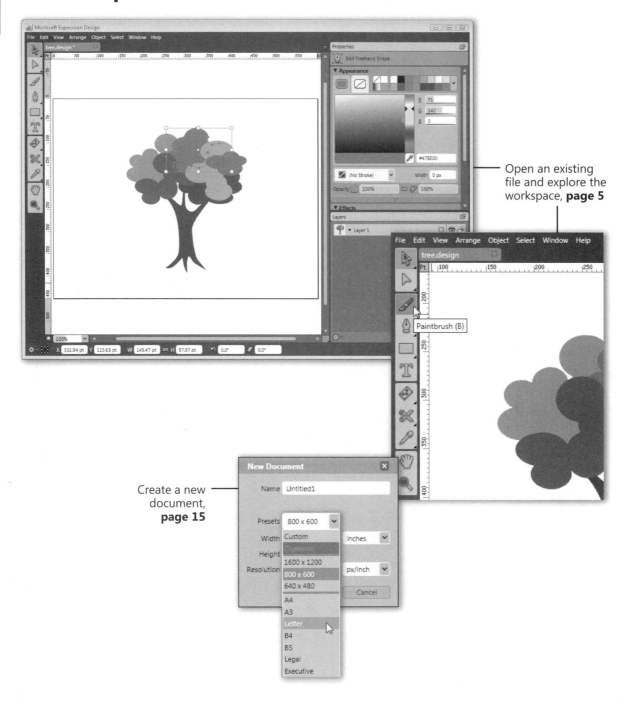

Open an existing file and explore the workspace, **page 5**

Create a new document, **page 15**

1 Working with Documents

In this chapter, you will learn to:

✔ Understand the difference between vector and raster.

✔ Open an existing file and explore the workspace.

✔ Create a new document.

✔ Import a document created in Creature House Expression versions 1–3.

Microsoft Expression Design is a unique illustration program with powerful tools for creative professionals and developers. In Expression Design, you can combine vector and raster graphics seamlessly for a large variety of effects and range of outputs, from application interfaces, the Web, or print. Illustrators, designers, and artists will find that Expression Design adds a powerful tool to their arsenal of programs.

In this chapter, you will learn the difference between vector and raster, and what it means to be able to work with both vector and raster elements in the same image. You will learn how to open an existing document and how to create a new document. You will also learn the different parts of the workspace, and learn to import documents created in Creature House Expression versions 1–3.

Important Before you can use the practice files in this chapter, you need to install them from the book's companion CD to their default location. For more information about practice files, see "Using the Book's CD" at the beginning of this book.

Troubleshooting Graphics and operating system–related instructions in this book reflect the Windows Vista user interface. If your computer is running Windows XP and you experience trouble following the instructions as written, please refer to the "Information for Readers Running Windows XP" section at the beginning of this book.

> **Important** In Expression Design, you can choose whether to work with a dark or light interface theme. The default is the Expression Design dark theme; screen shots in this book were taken with the Expression Design light theme. If you would like to change to the Expression Design light theme, point to Options on the Edit menu, and click Workspace. On the Theme menu, click Expression Light. Then click OK.

Understanding the Difference Between Vector and Raster

There are two types of graphic programs: those that are primarily for editing photos or painting, which are pixel-based and are called *paint*, *bitmap*, or *raster* programs; and those that are primarily for drawing, which are based on mathematical formulas and are called *illustration* or *vector* programs. When you begin to work with a program like Expression Design, which you can use to create and work with both vector and raster elements even within the same image, it is important to understand the differences and capabilities of both types of elements.

A **raster program** uses pixels to draw and paint. A **pixel** (short for *picture element*) is a tiny square of color. It is the smallest picture element of a **raster image**, much like an atom is the smallest element of matter. Photographs are an example of raster images. A photograph is made up of thousands of pixels of many different colors. At normal magnification, with the naked eye, you can't see the individual squares, and they meld together to form the shapes and colors within the image, creating smooth transitions from color to color and object to object. However, if you zoom in very close on a photograph or any other raster image, you can see the individual pixels.

An image has a finite number of pixels, which is determined by multiplying the number of pixels wide by the number of pixels high; for example, an image that measures 1600 pixels wide by 1200 pixels high contains 1,920,000 pixels. The print size for this image at 300 dots per inch (dpi, an ink measurement) is 6 inches by 4 inches. This means that each linear inch of printed space on the page will contain 300 dots of ink. If you enlarge this image but keep the same 300 dpi, the image has the same number of pixels, but they are stretched. The image becomes **pixilated**, resulting in jagged edges and blurry photos.

Adobe Photoshop, Adobe Photoshop Elements, Corel Painter, and Corel Paint Shop Pro are all considered raster programs. The images they create are referred to as *bitmap images* regardless of their actual file type. Common file name extensions for raster images include, but are not limited to, .jpeg, .bmp, .gif, and .tiff.

Programs like Expression Design, Adobe Illustrator, and CorelDRAW are **vector programs**, and the images created in them are called **vector graphics**, or simply *vectors* for short. These programs do not use pixels to define the images you see on the screen the way raster programs do; instead, they define what you see by using mathematical formulas. Vectors are composed of **paths**, consisting of **anchor points**, which are also called *nodes*, and the line segments between the anchor points. The line segments can be curved or straight. The graphic is stored as mathematical information: how many anchor points, their location on the page, their location in reference to each other, and how the line segment is connected between each anchor point. No matter how large or small the vector image is scaled, that information does not change, and the image will be as crisp and clear at 1 inch as it is at 100 inches—or 100 feet if you need it that large.

Common vector file name extensions include .ai, the native Illustrator format; .cdr, the format used by CorelDRAW; and .design, the native format for Expression Design.

Although most graphics programs are characterized as either raster or vector, that characterization refers to their primary function. Many programs allow users to combine raster and vector operations in one image. When saved in the program's native format, these images usually remain fully editable and retain the vector characteristics of any vector objects used in the image. As long as an Expression Design file is saved in the native .design format of Expression Design, all of the brush strokes and objects used will be fully editable. If you export the file to a raster image format, such as .bmp or .tiff, you can no longer edit any vector objects used in the image, and the image becomes a raster image.

What's the real difference between these formats, and why does it matter to you as a designer? If you create a company logo for business cards in a raster program such as Photoshop and later your client asks you to size the logo for use on a billboard, you will have to start over. Increasing the size of the existing logo will increase the size of the pixels and ruin your design. If you create the logo in vector format, you can make the image as large as necessary without losing any image quality.

The vector capabilities of Expression Design make it ideal for a designer, whatever the intended output. The images you create are perfect for print or the screen, or for using in other programs of the Microsoft Expression Studio.

Opening an Existing File and Exploring the Workspace

Each file you work with in Expression Design is called a ***document***. When Expression Design first starts, a blank, gray area called the ***workspace*** is displayed. This workspace has menus, a Toolbox, panels, and bars containing the tools for creating or editing a document.

Expression Design does not automatically open a new document in the workspace when you first start the program. Many features of the program are unavailable when no document is open, so your first task after starting the program is to open a document. You can open a blank document for a new project, or you can open a previously saved document to continue working.

Expression Design can open files in several formats. Supported formats, or file types, include the following:

- .psd (Photoshop 7 and earlier)

> **Tip** Be aware that although a .psd file might contain many layers, both raster and vector elements, text, and saved selections, the image will be flattened when opened in Expression Design.

- .tiff

> **Tip** A .tiff file might be layered and contain alpha channels, but the image will be flattened when opened in Expression Design. In bitmapped images with layers, ***alpha channels*** are the areas on a layer that are transparent. These channels can be loaded as ***masks*** or selections.

- .jpeg (or .jpg or .jfif)
- .gif
- .png
- .bmp (or .dib or .rle)
- .wdp or .hdp (Windows Media Photo or HD Photo)
- .ico

After you open a document, it appears in an area of the workspace called the *document window*. The document window is a virtually limitless area for drawing. As you get to the edge, the window scrolls to add more space for drawing.

Inside the document window is a *document frame* in the shape of the page. This frame is also called the *artboard*. Even though you have the area outside the artboard for drawing, anything drawn outside the boundaries of the artboard will not export or print, so it is often used as a repository for objects not on the artboard that you do not want to *delete* because you may need them later.

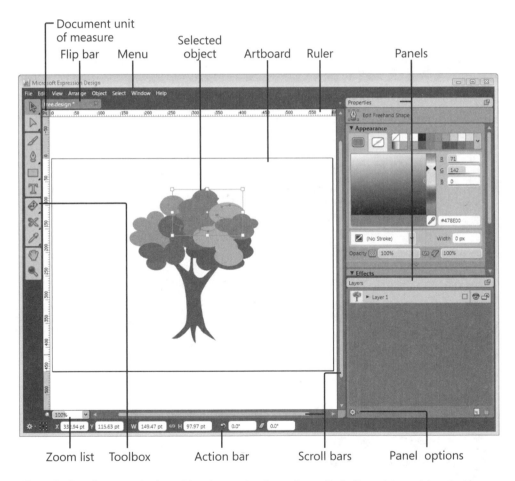

The window has vertical and horizontal rulers along its left and top sides. In the upper-left corner where the horizontal and vertical rulers meet, the unit of measurement used in the document is displayed; by default, this measurement is in pixels.

At the top of the document window is the *flip bar*, which shows the document name. Pointing to the name displays a ScreenTip with the location of the file on your hard disk. When a document has unsaved changes, an asterisk appears at the end of the file name on the flip bar. If more than one document is open, they each have their own tab on the flip bar, and you can navigate between the documents by clicking their tabs.

To create, select, and edit the paths and objects in the document, you use a collection of tools represented by icons in the *Toolbox*. Tools with a triangle in the lower-right corner of the icon are part of a tool group. To access the other tools in the group, point to the tool, and then click and hold to expose the tool group.

See Also For more information about the Toolbox, see "Using the Toolbox" in Chapter 2, "Navigating the Workspace."

To change image settings, such as the color of a path or object or the width of a brush stroke, you use the controls in the *Properties panel* and the *Layers panel*. You will find different kinds of controls, such as sliders, buttons, and scroll bars, which collectively are called *widgets*.

On the bottom of the artboard is the *Action Bar*, which gives information about a *selection*, such as the pivot point, x-coordinates and y-coordinates of the object on the artboard, the height and width of an object or objects, and the rotation or skew angle. It also gives you a fast way to change any of these options. The Action Bar is dynamic and changes according to the selection. If nothing is selected, it will be empty.

In this exercise, you will start Expression Design, explore the workspace, and practice opening a couple of existing files.

> **USE** the *pear.design* and *tree.design* files. These practice files are located in the *Documents\ Microsoft Press\Expression Design SBS\WorkingDocuments* folder.
> **BE SURE TO** start Expression Design before beginning this exercise.

1. On the **Start** menu, point to **All Programs**, click **Microsoft Expression**, and then click **Microsoft Expression Design**.

Expression Design displays the blank workspace.

> **Tip** The workspace is customizable, so to ensure your screen looks like the graphics in this chapter, click Reset Active Workspace on the Window menu.

2. On the **File** menu, click **Open** to open the **Open File** dialog box.

3. In the **Open File** dialog box, navigate to the *Documents\Microsoft Press\Expression Design SBS\WorkingDocuments* folder, click the *tree.design* file, and then click **Open**.

A tree illustration appears in the workspace. The components of this tree are called *objects*.

> **Tip** Most operations in Expression Design use the same keyboard shortcuts as Microsoft Office programs. In this case, you could also press Ctrl+O to open the Open File dialog box.

Within your workspace are the standard menus and commands you've seen in other programs. If you have previously used graphics software, many of the commands will be familiar to you.

4. Explore the commands on the menus.

Just like other Windows programs, keyboard shortcuts for those commands that have them are listed beside the command. Some commands are "grayed out," meaning that they are unavailable. This status is dynamic and changes based on the tool you are using and the active selections. An ellipsis (...) after a command means that clicking the command will open a dialog box with additional options.

Select	Window	Help
All		Ctrl+A
Deselect		Ctrl+Shift+A
Invert		Ctrl+Shift+I
Select By...		
Select Master		

5. Point to each icon in the Toolbox.

The currently active tool is always highlighted. Notice that as you point to an icon, its keyboard shortcut is displayed if the tool has one.

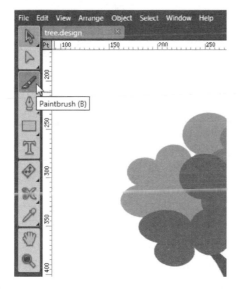

6. Move the mouse pointer over the document window.

As you move the pointer around the document window, notice that small lines appear on the rulers. These lines tell you the precise position of your pointer on the page and the path your pointer is on.

> **Tip** The upper-left corner of the page is the 0 point for both the x-coordinate (horizontal) and y-coordinate (vertical). This setting can be changed by clicking Set Document Origin on the File menu, and then clicking the spot on the document where you want to place the 0,0 point.

The unit of measurement can be changed to suit the intended output of the document or your preference.

7. On the **Edit** menu, click **Options**, and then in the left pane of the **Options** dialog box, click **Units and Grids**. In the **Document Units** list, click **inches**, and then click **OK** to accept the change.

Options

General	**Units**	
Workspace	Document units	points
Stroke	Stroke units	inches
Display	Type units	millimeters
Units and Grids		centimeters
Files		picas
Clipboard (XAML)	**Grids and guides**	points
Print and Export	Grid size	pixels
Memory and Undo		

Rulers

☑ Ruler origin is always top left of artboard

Arrangement

Rotation steps	8
Nudge increment	0.75 pt
Stack gap size	7.5 pt

OK   Cancel

8. Move the pointer to the top of the document window to examine the flip bar.

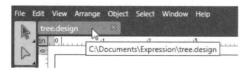

9. To the right of the workspace, explore the panels.

When you first open Expression Design, two panels are open, Properties and Layers. Do not think that this means there aren't very many controls! In these two panels are some of the most important tools you will use in Expression Design. From these panels, you control the colors, fills and blend modes of strokes and objects, brush strokes and their widths, the *opacity* of strokes and fills, and even how lines are drawn. These panels are dynamic, so as other tools are used and other objects are selected, the content of the panels change to give you more tools and options. The Layers panel gives you the freedom to isolate elements of your design on their own layers. As you work through the exercises in this book, you will come to appreciate the power of layers, probably more than any other feature of Expression Design.

Above the panels, the tool currently selected in the Toolbox and its use is displayed. Currently, the Selection tool is active. If you click any one of the green leaf objects with the Selection tool, the object is highlighted. To edit any path or object, you must select the object by using the Selection tool. Operations you perform only affect selected paths and objects.

> **Tip** The keyboard shortcut for the Selection tool is V. You might not be a fan of keyboard shortcuts, but if you only learn one, this should be it. You will use this tool often!

10. Using the **Selection** tool, click the green leaf object shown surrounded by an outline in this graphic:

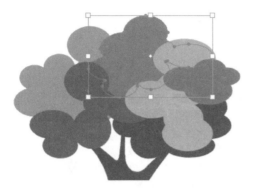

Notice that the red dots and outline you see in your program window indicate the anchor points and segments that make up the shape, and that the outline shows the shape even if it is behind another one. The leaf shape is also surrounded by a blue rectangular bounding box with edit handles.

Objects that are selected can be manipulated in a variety of ways. By simply dragging selected objects or groups of objects with the Selection tool, you can reposition them on the page.

11. Drag any of the leaf objects, and then move it back.

Objects can also be resized, rotated, or skewed by using the handles on the bounding box, skills that will be covered in Chapter 3, "Manipulating Objects," or they can be completely reshaped by using the Direct Selection tool on the anchor points. When anchor points are selected independently of the shape, they have their own handles that you can use to determine exactly how the segment between the anchor points behaves. That statement may have you shaking your head, but when we work on editing anchor points and objects in Chapter 5, "Using the Drawing Tools," you will find out just how versatile these nodes and their handles really are.

12. With the leaf object selected, look at the values in the boxes on the Action Bar. Then, using the **Selection** tool, click the tree trunk.

Notice that the values in the boxes have changed to reflect the position and size of the tree trunk object.

X 4.198 in   Y 5.91 in   W 2.218 in   H 3.34 in   0.0°   0.0°

13. If the trunk is still selected, hold down the ⎡Shift⎤ key and click one of the leaf objects to add it to the selection. If the trunk is not selected, hold down the ⎡Shift⎤ key, click the trunk, and then click one of the leaf objects.

> **Tip** You can also use the Selection tool to drag a marquee around several paths or objects to select them as a group.

When more than one path or object is selected, several things change. In the Action Bar, you now have options for aligning, changing the *stacking order* (the order in which the objects appear from front to back on the page), and performing path operations. Both paths show the anchor points and segments in red, and both show the bounding box. These two paths can now be edited at the same time; for example, changing the color changes the color for both paths at once.

14. On the **File** menu, click **Open**, and then open the *pear.design* file.

Two tabs appear on the flip bar: one for *tree.design*, and one for *pear.design*. No matter how many open images you have, each one will have its own tab on the flip bar.

15. Click the **tree.design** tab to bring that document to the front.

When you have several documents open, the flip bar will usually have room for all of the image tabs to be visible. If you have so many documents open that there isn't room for all the tabs on the flip bar, some may be hidden.

16. At the right end of the flip bar (just to the left of the Properties panel), click the arrow to display a list of the open documents, and then click the document you want to bring to the front.

The list shows a check mark by the name of the active document.

Tip You can press Ctrl+Tab to switch to the next document on the flip bar, or press Ctrl+Shift+Tab to switch to the previous document.

17. Close the active document by clicking the **X** on its tab, or by clicking **Close** on the **File** menu.

Close

Tip You can close all the open documents at once by clicking Close All on the File menu.

CLOSE all documents by clicking Close All on the File menu.

Creating a New Document

Many times, you will want to start a new document from scratch so that it is based on the intended output for the final artwork. Because Expression Design is a multi-use program, you can create artwork for three kinds of output: print, Web, or media.

In this exercise, you will create a new document in Expression Design. There are no practice files for this exercise.

BE SURE TO start Expression Design if you closed it previously.

1. On the **File** menu, click **New**.

The New Document dialog box opens so that you can save time by making several choices for the document before it is created.

2. In the **Name** box, type a name for the document if you want.

This name is used by default when the document is saved later. If you prefer, you can assign the file name at the time you save the file.

3. From the **Presets** list, choose a size for the new document.

This setting determines the size of the artboard and the printable size of the document. The list of preset sizes includes common sizes for common outputs, such as Web and paper.

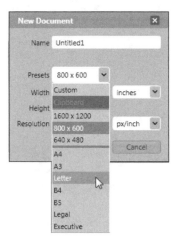

> **Tip** The Letter preset has the portrait orientation. If you want to work on a document that has the landscape orientation, select Letter, and then switch the sizes in the Width and Height boxes manually. You can also wait until the document opens and rotate it by pointing to Rotate Document on the File menu and then clicking Rotate 90° Clockwise or Rotate 90° Counter Clockwise.

If the size you want is not in the Presets list, you can select a custom size by clicking a unit of measurement in the Units list to the right of the Width box and then entering the preferred sizes in the Width and Height boxes.

For this exercise, we will create a half-page document by using inches.

4. Display the **Units** list, click **inches** if it's not already selected, and then enter a **Width** of **5.5** and a **Height** of **8.5**.

The abbreviation for the unit of measurement (in this case, *in*) is added for you. The size you choose remains set for all subsequent new documents until you change it in the New Document dialog box.

The final choice you need to make when creating a new document is its resolution. Because you will usually be creating vector elements in Expression Design, you might think that resolution doesn't matter. (As you learned in the first part of this chapter, vectors are stored as mathematical formulas and can be resized at will without any loss of quality.) However, you do need to select a resolution when you create a new document because the value you choose not only determines the document's native resolution but also sets the resolution at which live effects will be rasterized. (**Live effects** are bitmap effects, and the term **rasterized** means converting into a bitmap format.) So it is important to set the resolution high enough for its intended output.

> **Tip** Some live effects are resolution-dependent, so if you change the resolution later, the effect could look different. In that case, you can reapply the effect. Live effects can be added, removed, and altered at any time.

5. If you plan to print the document, type a resolution of 300 or higher. If the document is for the Web, a resolution of 72 or 96 will suffice.

For this exercise, it isn't important which resolution you choose.

6. Click **OK** to close the **New Document** dialog box and create the new document.

CLOSE the document you created for this exercise.

Importing a Document Created in Creature House Expression Versions 1–3

If you have used a previous incarnation of Expression Design, you might have files you would like to open in the current version. You can open .xpr files created in earlier versions of Expression Design, including the Community Technology Preview (CTP) versions; Creature House Expression 1, 2, and 3; and Microsoft Acrylic 3. Be aware, however, that some features are no longer supported, and you might lose some aspects of your design. For example, the following image, which was created in Expression 3, uses several features no longer supported, such as fringes and textures.

Here are the general steps for importing a file:

1. On the **File** menu, click **Open**. Then in the **Open** dialog box, navigate to the file you want to import, and double-click it.

The Import Document dialog box opens, letting you know there may be some problems importing the file because some features are not supported.

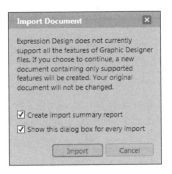

This dialog box provides the following options:

- If you choose to open the file, Expression Design creates a new document by using only the supported features and preserves your original file.
- If you want a report of what features were removed, you can select the Create Import Summary Report check box.
- If you want to see this dialog box every time you import a file, you can select the Show This Dialog Box For Every Import check box.

2. Click **Import** to open the file.

   If the document uses only supported features, a dialog box telling you that there are no changes appears.

3. Click the **Close** button to close the dialog box and complete the import.

Close

   Your image should look the same as it did when it was originally created.

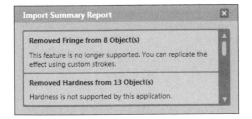

If the document uses features that are no longer supported, a dialog box listing the features that have been removed appears.

4. Scroll though the list in the dialog box to see which features have been removed and look for ideas about how to replicate the original effect.

5. Click the **Close** button to close the report and complete the import.

    Depending on which non-supported features were used in the original image, the imported image might look very different or much the same. Expression Design opens a copy of these older files to preserve the original document. Some non-supported features from previous versions of Expression Design might return in future versions.

The wolf image used textures, fringes, and several other features, so the imported image is very different from the original file.

CLOSE all open documents. If you are not continuing directly on to the next chapter, exit Expression Design.

Key Points

- The workspace consists of menus containing commands, a Toolbox containing tools, panels containing widgets, and the document window. This is where you will open, edit, and save documents. All of the tools you need for illustration are in this workspace.

- Previously saved files can be opened so that you can continue working on them.

- New files can be created with options you select at the time you create the file. You can name the file, and choose the size of the document from preset or custom sizes. You are also able to set the resolution that will be used when the file is rasterized, and the unit of measurement you would like to use: pixels, inches, or centimeters based on the intended output for your illustration.

- Documents created in Creature House Expression versions 1–3 can be opened in Expression Design, even if some features are no longer supported. A copy of the file will be opened so that you can retain the original document. It is possible that currently unsupported features will return in future versions of Expression Design.

Chapter at a Glance

Use the Toolbox, **page 24**

Use panels and panel widgets, **page 28**

Change the display and preview modes, **page 34**

Use the Zoom tool, **page 41**

2 Navigating the Workspace

In this chapter, you will learn to:

✔ Use the Toolbox, panels, panel widgets, and the Zoom tool.

✔ Change the display and preview modes.

✔ Move around in a document.

✔ Undo mistakes.

✔ Save your work.

Microsoft Expression Design offers many tools for drawing paths and shapes, painting paths with customizable brushes, and using various fills and strokes, as well as working with bitmaps. These tools have many settings, and by the end of this chapter, you will know how to access the settings and what they control.

Expression Design provides several ways of moving around in and viewing documents that can make working in the program easier and more efficient. Using the *Undo* and *Revert* commands to go back in time, saving documents, and understanding the Auto Save and rescue files features can make the difference between starting over completely and going back to just before you made the big mistake.

In this chapter, you will learn to use all the features just described. First, you will use the Toolbox, panels, panel widgets, and Zoom tool. Then you'll learn to set *display quality*, rotate the viewing area, navigate documents, and undo mistakes. You will also explore the Auto Save and rescue files features, and save your work.

> **Important** Before you can use the practice files in this chapter, you need to install them from the book's companion CD to their default location. See "Using the Book's CD" at the beginning of this book for more information.

> **Troubleshooting** Graphics and operating system–related instructions in this book reflect the Windows Vista user interface. If your computer is running Windows XP and you experience trouble following the instructions as written, please refer to the "Information for Readers Running Windows XP" section at the beginning of this book.

Using the Toolbox

In Chapter 1, "Working with Documents," you learned where the Toolbox is. Throughout this chapter, you will learn how to access the tools in the Toolbox and how to alter their settings.

The Toolbox contains the tools you need to create and edit your drawings. Related tools are grouped together, and some tools are grouped into tool groups. Tool groups are tools that occupy the same space in the Toolbox. Tools containing tool groups have a triangle to indicate that other tools are hidden beneath them. If a tool has a marker in the lower-right corner, you can press and hold either the left or right mouse button to expand the tool group.

The Toolbox also contains all the tools you need to create and edit paths and navigate documents in Expression Design. It is divided into the following four sections containing related tools:

- Selection tools
- Tools for creating paths, shapes, and text
- Tools for manipulating the colors and shapes of paths and objects
- Toolbox tools used for document navigation

Other related tools are stored beneath the default tools in *tool groups*.

In this exercise, you will use the Toolbox tools to edit a picture. You will also change the stacking order of objects on the page.

> **USE** the *tree.design* file. This practice file is located in the *Documents\Microsoft Press\Expression Design SBS\NavigatingWorkspace* folder.
> **BE SURE TO** start Expression Design before beginning this exercise.
> **OPEN** the *tree.design* file.

1. Look at the Toolbox, which is along the left edge of the workspace.

Line

2. Click and hold the **Line** tool to expand the tool group.

Rectangle

3. In the tool group, click (don't double-click) the **Rectangle** tool to select it.

> **Tip** You can point to any tool to display its keyboard shortcut.

Using the Rectangle tool, you will add some ground under the tree.

4. Drag in the document to draw a rectangle at the base of the tree.

When you release the mouse button, the rectangle fills with the currently selected fill color (the color that you used most recently, or white if no other color has been selected).

5. In the **Appearance** group on the Properties panel, click the **Fill** tab, and then click the red square to change the fill color to red.

Now you will be able to see the rectangle when we move it behind the tree.

Notice that because the rectangle was drawn after the tree trunk, the rectangle is in front of the trunk and obscures it from view.

6. To position the rectangle so that it is behind the tree, right-click the rectangle, click **Arrange**, and then click **Send to Back**.

The rectangle moves behind the tree, changing the stacking order.

> **Tip** Bring Forward moves the selected object ahead of the next one in the stacking order. Send To Back moves the selected object behind all objects so that it is lowest in the stacking order, and Bring To Front brings the selected object to the front of the stacking order.

7. If you need to move the rectangle, click the **Selection** tool in the Toolbox. Then select the rectangle and drag it to its new position.

8. On the **File** menu, click **Save As**. In the **Save As** dialog box, enter **treedesign2** in the **File name** box, and then click **OK**.

9. Select any three objects on the tree, then on the **Action Bar**, in the **Stack** menu, click **To the Right**.

Note how the objects snap into position.

10. Press Ctrl+Z to undo the stack, and then repeat step 9, selecting the **Downward** option.

> **BE SURE TO** click Revert on the File menu to undo the changes and revert to your saved version of the *tree.design2* document, when you are done experimenting.

Stacking Order

The order in which objects or paths are added to the document determines their order on the page. This is called the *stacking order.* As objects are added to the page, they are placed in front of objects already on the page. The order can be changed by right-clicking an object with the Selection tool and clicking an option on the Arrange menu, or by clicking Order on the Arrange menu, and then clicking the option you want.

When multiple objects or an object group is selected, the Action Bar displays a Stack list. You might assume that options on this list change the stacking order. However, they work differently. The options on the Action Bar Stack list change the position of the objects on the page, anchoring one object and distributing the others an equal distance apart in the direction you choose, rather than changing their stacking order.

- **Upward** anchors the bottommost object and moves the others so that they are distributed equal distances apart vertically upward.

- **Downward** anchors the topmost object and moves the others so that they are distributed equal distances apart vertically downward.

- **To The Left** anchors the rightmost object and moves the others so that they are distributed equal distances apart horizontally to the left.

- **To The Right** anchors the leftmost object and moves the others so that they are distributed equal distances apart horizontally to the right.

Using Panels and Panel Widgets

As you saw in Chapter 1, the Toolbox is one of the four context-sensitive control areas in the workspace that provide the features you need to create and modify objects and illustrations. The other areas are the Properties panel, the Layers panel, and the Action Bar, which appears only when a document is open.

By default, the panels are docked in a *pane* to the right of the workspace.

To work with panels, you can do the following:

- Open and close panels by choosing them from the Window menu.

- To give yourself more room to work, hide all panels on the screen by pressing the Tab key. Press Tab again to bring them back.

● Point to the left edge of the vertical pane in which the Layers and Properties
  panels are docked, and when the pointer changes to a double-headed arrow,
  drag to resize the pane.

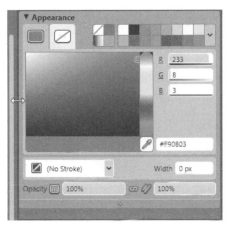

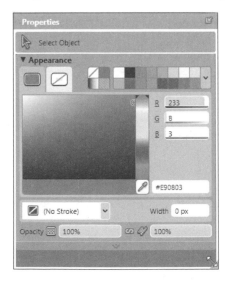
Float

● Click once on the panel's Float button (located in the upper-right corner of the
  panel) to remove the panel from the pane and *float* it in the workspace. When
  a panel is floating, the Float button becomes the Dock button.

● Drag the title bar of a panel in Float mode to place the panel anywhere on your screen.

● If you are working with a dual-monitor setup, drag a floating panel to the second
  monitor.

● Drag the Resize area in the lower-right corner of a floating panel to resize it.

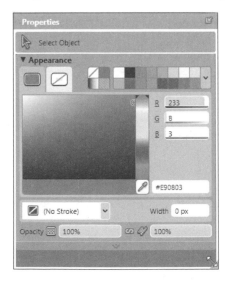

● Click the Dock button to *dock*, or *pin*, the panel to the pane, which is its default
  location.

Panels have the following characteristics:

- **They are context-sensitive.** The term *context-sensitive* means that the options and content of the panel change according to the tool that is selected in the Toolbox. In the following graphic, the Text tool is the active tool. The Properties panel shows this in two ways: the tool is shown at the top of the panel, and the options available are related to working with text. Because context-sensitive panels change content when you change the selected tool, options for your current tool choice are readily available.

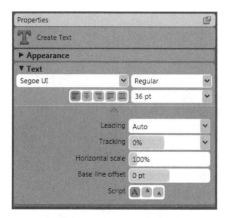

- **They contain widgets.** The Expression Design panels contain *sliders* and *buttons* that give you a lot of flexibility for setting options to manipulate paths and shapes. Collectively, these controls are called widgets. It's important for you to know how they work so you can maximize your editing power in Expression Design.

  - Sliders are useful for quickly fine-tuning the values of attributes. Many sliders first appear as text or a number, but when you point to them, the pointer changes to a four-headed arrow.

  - Buttons represent a link to additional information. Expression Design sometimes hides editing options to fit the panel into the allotted space. The following two types of More Information buttons indicate hidden features:

    ▶ Click this type of More Information button to expand or collapse a category.

    ⌄ Click this type of More Information button to open advanced settings for a section in the panel.

● **They can be scrolled.** When there is more content in a panel than room to display it, a *scroll bar* appears along the right side of the panel. You can use the scroll bar in the following ways to navigate the contents of a long panel:

   ● Click and hold the arrows at the top or bottom of the scroll bar to move the contents of the panel up or down.

   ● Click the scroll bar and drag it to move the contents you need into view.

   ● Right-click the scroll bar and choose an option from the context menu.

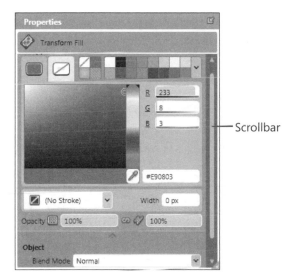

Scrollbar

In this exercise, you will use the panels and panel widgets to edit an image in a document.

USE the *treedesign2* file you created in the previous exercise.
OPEN the *tree.design2* file if it is not already open.

1. Select a tree leaf. In the **Appearance** panel, click a color swatch to change the color of the fill of the leaf.

2. Change the colors of several other leaves or the trunk.

3. Select any leaf. On the **Action Bar**, point to the **X** slider until the pointer changes to a four-headed arrow. Then click and drag to change the x-coordinate value in the box and move the selected object.

4. On the **Action Bar**, point to the **W** (width) slider, and click and drag when you see the double-headed arrow.

The width of the selected object changes. If the chain icon is connected between the **W** and **H** sliders, the object will be resized in both width and height, in proportion. To change only the width or the height, click the link to break it.

| W | 181.2 pt | ∞ | H | 104.75 pt |

> **Tip** You can type precise values into the W and H sliders on the Action Bar to control the size or position of selected objects.

5. On the **File** menu, click **Revert** to discard all changes to *tree.design2*. Click the red rectangle we created in the previous procedure to select it.

   The Properties panel now says Edit Rectangle.

   | Properties | |
   | Edit Rectangle | |

6. Drag the **Opacity** slider to change the opacity of the rectangle 1 percent at a time.

   The appearance of the rectangle is updated in real time, so you can adjust it precisely.

   > **Tip** Holding the Shift key as you drag adjusts the setting in higher increments. Instead of 1 percent, the setting is adjusted by 10 percent.

7. Drag the corner of the rectangle to resize it.

   Notice that as you resize by dragging, the Action Bar shows the new size of the rectangle.

8. Select the tree leaves and the trunk. A quick way to do this is to click **All** on the **Select** menu, and then hold down the ⎡shift⎤ key and click the rectangle to remove it from the selection.

   > **Tip** Ctrl+A is the keyboard shortcut to select all items on a page. You might find this more convenient than using the Select menu.

   In the Appearance panel, notice that the Stroke list says (No Stroke) and stroke width is set to 0.

   | ☑ (No Stroke) | ⌄ | Width | 0 px |

9. Type **10** in the **Width** box. Then press Enter to set the stroke width to 10 pixels. Choose the basic stroke from the Stroke Gallery to apply the stroke to the selected objects.

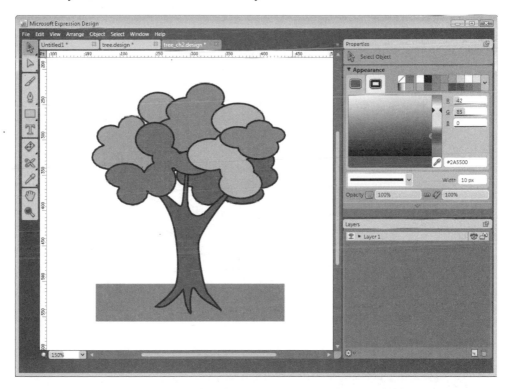

10. Click away from the tree to *deselect* it so you can see the strokes.

See Also Expression Design's strokes feature is one of its most useful. In Chapter 7, "Using Strokes," you will learn to use these strokes to your advantage and see how changing the type of stroke can change the entire mood of an illustration.

BE SURE TO click Reset Active Workspace on the Window menu to return any floating panels to the right pane before continuing.

CLOSE the *treedesign2* file without saving any changes.

Changing the Display and Preview Modes

When working in Expression Design, you can choose from three views of your documents: *Path view*, *Wireframe* view, and Preview view. These display options affect only how the document is displayed on your screen; they do not affect the output in any way.

In Chapter 1, we discussed the differences between vector and raster. With Pixel Preview mode, you can see what your illustration would look like if it were rasterized. Your illustration will remain a vector illustration, but Pixel Preview will help you visualize the output in a rasterized format so that you can fix any problems before final output.

You can look at the same document in more than one window by creating a new view. This enables you to zoom in to work up close in one view, while remaining zoomed out in another view so that you can see the effects of your modifications on the entire illustration. You are not making a *duplicate* of the document, merely viewing the same document twice from a different point of view.

You can view your illustration in portrait or landscape mode, but a straightforward portrait or landscape orientation might not always provide you with the best angle to work on your illustration, particularly if you use a graphics tablet rather than a mouse.

Think about drawing on a piece of paper: many people rotate the paper for a more natural drawing angle. With Expression Design, you can do the same thing by rotating the viewing area.

To rotate the viewing area, you use the Rotate View Clockwise or Rotate View Counter Clockwise command on the View menu to rotate the page in the corresponding direction. As with the other display settings, rotating the viewing area affects only the way you view your document on the screen; it does not affect the output in any way.

In this exercise, you will experiment with views and preview modes and rotate the viewing area without rotating the document.

USE the *pear.design* file. This practice file is located in the *Documents\Microsoft Press\ Expression Design SBS\NavigatingWorkspace* folder.

OPEN the *pear.design* file.

Tip If you used the *pear.design* file in Chapter 1, it might be on the File menu under Recent Files. To open a file you worked on recently, click Recent Files on the File menu, and then click the file you want. The full path to the file is shown, so you can see where it is stored.

1. Verify that the document is in the default *Preview* mode. If it is not in Preview
mode, click **Display Quality** on the **View** menu, and then click **Preview**.

> **Tip** You can tell if a document is in Preview mode because you will see your drawing
> as you intended, with fills and strokes and colors.

In Preview mode, the colors of the pear and stem are visible. The full width, shape,
color, and varying opacity of the watercolor strokes that make up the background
are also visible. In Preview, your document looks very similar to the final output.

2. On the **View** menu, click **Display Quality**, and then click **Wireframe**.

Wireframe view shows the outer shape of the strokes and shapes in a black outline.
This view is very useful when you want to select a path that is below another one
in the stacking order, or when strokes overlap to the point where it is difficult to
select the one you want.

3. In the **Layers** panel, click **Layer 1** to make that layer active.

This illustration has only one layer, but often an illustration has many layers, and you must always make sure you are working on the correct one.

Layer Options

4. At the bottom of the **Layers** panel, click the Layer Options icon. In the menu that appears, click **Layer Options**, click **Layer Render Style**, and then click **Path**.

Path view is available only on a layer-by-layer basis. You can now see the skeleton of all of the paths that make up the pear illustration. They appear as one-pixel black strokes, without showing the actual width or shapes of any of the strokes.

5. Change **Layer Render Style** back to **Default** before continuing with step 6.

The Layer Render Style settings will override the settings on the Display Quality menu if you do not do so.

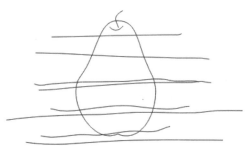

6. Click **Display Quality** on the View menu, and then click **Preview** to return to Preview mode before continuing.

7. On the **View** menu, click **Pixel Preview** to turn on Pixel Preview mode.

8. In the **Pixel Preview** dialog box, under **Rasterization**, use the sliders to set the desired size and resolution.

9. Under **File format**, in the **File type** and **Mode** lists, click the options you want. What you choose will depend on whether you want to print the image or save it for the Web. These options will show you an approximation of what the image would look like in final output. They do not change any settings.

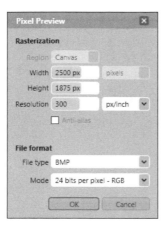

10. Click **OK**.

11. Return to Preview mode by clicking **Pixel Preview** on the **View** menu to toggle off Pixel Preview mode.

12. At the bottom of the **View** menu, click **New View**.

A second tab appears at the top of the document.

13. Click the tabs to toggle between the two views.

Until you make changes to one of the views, they will look identical.

pear.design:1   pear.design:2

14. Click the **pear.design:2** tab.

15. On the **View** menu, click **Zoom In**.

16. On the **pear.design:1** tab, click the pear by using the **Selection** tool, and then drag it on the page.

17. Switch to the **pear.design:2** tab to verify that the pear has also moved position in the second view.

18. On the **File** menu, click **Revert**.

19. In the **Revert To Saved** message box, click **Yes** to return the *pear.design* file to its previously saved state.

You will still have two views.

> **Tip** If you use a stylus on a graphics tablet, you can draw with a more natural feel and movement than you can with a mouse, and it allows for pressure and tilt. The stylus becomes an extension of your hand.

20. Click the **pear.design:1** tab at the top of the document.

21. On the **View** menu, click **Rotate View Clockwise** to rotate the page.

22. Click the **pear.design:2** tab.

Notice that the viewing area has not rotated in the second view.

23. Click the **pear.design:1** tab to return to the first document.

24. On the **View** menu, click **Reset View Rotation** to straighten the view.

25. Click the **Close** button (the **x**) on the **pear.design:2** tab to close that view.

> **CLOSE** the *pear.design* file if you are not continuing directly on to the next topic. Otherwise, leave it open.

Moving Around in a Document

As discussed in "Opening an Existing File and Exploring the Workspace" in Chapter 1, you can use the flip bar to navigate among open documents. When only one document is open, there are several ways to move around in it.

When a document is too large to be displayed completely in the workspace, or when you have zoomed in to see an object better, you can bring the area you would like to work with into view in the following ways:

- **Scroll bars.** These behave like the scroll bars do in most Windows applications. You can drag a scroll bar back and forth or up and down to see the rest of the document. You can also click a scroll arrow to move the scroll bar in that direction.

  > **Tip** Because the workspace is virtually limitless in Expression Design, you can use the arrows to scroll past the end of the document. You can store elements you would like to save for later use outside of the printable area, the edge of which is indicated by the document boundary.

- **Pan tool.** This tool in the Toolbox not only looks like a hand, it acts like one, letting you drag the document around in the window.

  > **Tip** Although you can always activate the Pan tool by clicking it in the Toolbox, you might find it more efficient to activate it by pressing the H key (which you can remember by using the mnemonic "H is for Hand"). To activate the Pan tool temporarily, hold down the Spacebar. Double-click the Pan tool in the Toolbox to view the document at its actual size.

- **Mouse wheel.** If your mouse has a wheel, it is set to zoom in and out of the page by default in Expression Design. The center of the zoom area is the position of the mouse pointer.

  > **Tip** If you want to change the default settings, click Options on the Edit menu, and then click General. Under Mouse Wheel, clear the Mouse Wheel Zoom About Mouse Position check box so that scrolling with the mouse wheel will always default to the center of the document. If you prefer the mouse wheel to scroll vertically or horizontally rather than zoom, click the appropriate option in the Mouse Wheel Usage list.

● **Menu commands.** As with all programs, Expression Design has many common tasks that are easily reached through the menus. These include basic tasks, such as opening, saving, and closing files; as well as commands to manipulate objects. Many menu commands are also available in tool settings in the panels or on the Action Bar; use the methods that best fit your needs.

In this exercise, you will move around in a document by scrolling, panning, and zooming.

USE the *pear.design* file you worked with in the previous exercise. This practice file is located in the *Documents\Microsoft Press\Expression Design SBS\NavigatingWorkspace* folder.

OPEN the *pear.design* file, if it is not already open.

1. Click **Zoom In** on the **View** menu.

You should see scroll bars on the right side and bottom of the document window.

2. Try scrolling by using the scroll bars and the arrows.

Pan

3. Click the **Pan** tool in the Toolbox, and try dragging the document in the window.

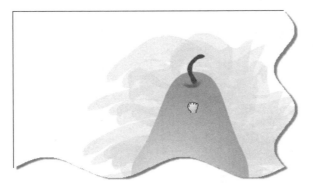

4. Point to an area of the *pear.design* file that you want to zoom, and then roll the wheel forward to zoom in and backward to zoom out.

5. On the **View** menu, try each of the options. Click **Fit to Screen** to view the entire document in the window, **Actual Size** to view the document at its true dimensions, and **Center View** to center the document in the window. Also try **Zoom In**, **Zoom Out**, and **Zoom To Selection**. Zoom To Selection is only available if something on the page is selected.

CLOSE the *pear.design* file if you are not continuing directly on to the next topic. Otherwise, leave it open.

Using the Zoom Tool

Any portion of the viewing area can be magnified up to 6400 percent or zoomed out to about 3 percent of normal size. You have already seen how you can use the mouse wheel or View menu commands to zoom. Another option is to use the Zoom tool.

In this exercise, you will use the Zoom tool to change the viewing area of your document.

USE the *pear.design* file you worked with in the previous exercise. This practice file is located in the *Documents\Microsoft Press\Expression Design SBS\NavigatingWorkspace* folder.

OPEN the *pear.design* file, if it is not already open.

1. In the Toolbox, click the **Zoom** tool.

2. Click anywhere in the view area to zoom in.

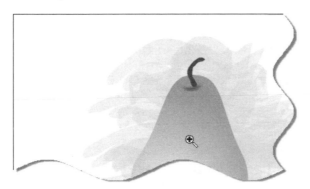

3. Hold down the Alt key as you click to zoom out.

4. In the lower-left corner of the image window, click the arrow next to the magnification number to show the **Zoom** list, from which you can choose preset zoom levels.

Expression Design always displays the current view magnification. In addition to a number of preset zoom percentages, you can choose Actual Pixels, Fit To Selected, Fit To Canvas, or Fit To Screen from the list.

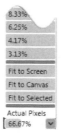

> **Tip** You can double-click the Zoom tool in the Toolbox to fit the document to the available window size. This will make the document fill the window; It will be as large as possible without scroll bars. To quickly zoom in on a specific area of a document, click the Zoom tool in the Toolbox, and then drag to select the area you want to zoom.

> **CLOSE** the *pear.design* file if you are not continuing directly on to the next topic. Otherwise, leave it open.

Undoing Mistakes

You can reverse the changes you make to any document. You can either undo one change at a time or remove all changes at once, reverting the document to the stage at which the last save occurred.

> **Tip** Undo and *Redo* have keyboard shortcuts, which are often faster to use than the menu commands. The keyboard shortcut for Undo is Ctrl+Z, which reverses the last change made to the document. To reverse multiple changes, press Ctrl+Z repeatedly. This reverses changes in the order in which they were made. The keyboard shortcut for Redo is Ctrl+Shift+Z, which reverses the last Undo action.

Changing the Number of Undo Steps

By default, Expression Design remembers 40 undo steps, but you can change that number to as many as 200 on the Memory And Undo panel of the Options dialog box. To change the number of undo levels, on the File menu, click Options, and then click Memory And Undo. Enter the desired number of Undo levels. The changes will not take effect until the next time Expression Design is started.

In this exercise, you will undo and redo changes to a file.

> **USE** the *pear.design* file you worked with in the previous exercise. This practice file is located in the *Documents\Microsoft Press\Expression Design SBS\NavigatingWorkspace* folder.
> **OPEN** the *pear.design* file, if it is not already open.

1. In the **Toolbox**, click the **Selection** tool. Then drag the pear image to a new location in the document.

2. On the **Arrange** menu, click **Transform**, and then click **Rotate 90° Clockwise**.

3. To reverse only the last action, on the **Edit** menu, click **Undo**.

Because the last action was Rotate 90° Clockwise, you should see Undo Rotate as the first entry on the Edit menu.

4. Click **Undo Rotate** to undo the rotation.

Viewing the Edit menu again displays Undo Translate and Redo Rotate.

5. On the **Edit** menu, click **Redo Rotate**.

6. This time, on the **Edit** menu, click **Undo Rotate**, and then **Undo Translate**.

7. On the **Edit** menu, click **Redo Translate**, and then click **Redo Rotate**.

8. To cancel all changes since the last save, click **Revert** on the **File** menu, and then click **Yes**.

This returns the document to the state it was in when it was last saved.

CLOSE the *pear.design* file. If you are not continuing directly to the next chapter, exit Expression Design.

Understanding Auto Save and Rescue Files

Expression Design has a built-in safeguard against system or program error: it periodically saves the open document as a rescue file. Rescue files are saved in Expression Design's native file format, .design. To avoid filling your hard drive with rescue versions of the same document, Expression Design removes these files whenever you save or close the document.

When you start Expression Design after a program or system error, it automatically opens any current rescue files.

> **Tip** Although the Auto Save and rescue files features in Expression Design can help salvage a document, they are not substitutes for regularly saving your files. Any time you work, you should make it a habit to save your documents frequently.

To set options for Auto Save, click Options on the Edit menu, and then click Files. There are several Native Format Save Options in the Autosave Frequency list. You can choose from Never, Seldom (about every 5 minutes), Normal (about every 30 seconds), or Frequent (about every 5 seconds). The default is Normal.

Saving Your Work

Expression Design saves documents in its native file format, .design. This format retains all layers, strokes, and other elements specific to the program. As a safeguard against losing your work, Expression Design asks if you want to save the changes when you try to close a document that has not been saved.

To save your document, click Save on the File menu. If you are saving the file for the first time, a dialog box opens so that you can choose where you want the file saved. Navigate to the folder of your choice, and type the file name. Then click the Save button.

After making further edits to the document, you can simply click Save on the File menu. The new version of the document will overwrite the previous one.

> **Tip** The keyboard shortcut for the Save command is Ctrl+S.

To save your document with a new name, click Save As on the File menu. The Save As dialog box opens so that you can choose where you want the file to be saved. Navigate to the folder of your choice, and type the new file name. Then click the Save button.

> **Tip** The keyboard shortcut for the Save As command is Ctrl+Shift+S.

To save a copy of the current state of a document without affecting the document you are working on, click Save A Copy on the File menu. Type a new name for the document in the Save dialog box, and then click Save.

> **Tip** The keyboard shortcut for the Save A Copy command is Ctrl+Alt+S.

Exporting Files in Other File Formats

Files can be exported in a variety of other file formats. Other file formats will be discussed in Chapter 10, "Exporting and Printing Your Work." Although these other formats are great for sharing your work, you lose the ability to edit layers, change strokes, and many other features that make Expression Design so versatile. So you should always retain a copy of your file in the native Expression Design format.

Key Points

- The Toolbox contains all the tools you need to create and edit paths and to navigate documents. Some of these tools have other related tools beneath them. These are called *tool groups*.

- Panels are docked at the side of the workspace by default, but you can float them anywhere in the workspace by clicking the Float button.

- Use scroll bars to display information when the panel is not long or wide enough for its contents.

- By setting Display Quality options, you can choose how paths and objects are displayed. Add New Views to be able to work in several zoom levels at once. To work on a more natural angle, particularly when using a graphics tablet, rotate the viewing area from the View menu.

- When a document is too large to display completely in the workspace, or when you have zoomed in closer to see an object better, you can move around in the document and bring into view the area you would like to edit. You can do this by using the Pan and Zoom tools, the View menu, or by using the mouse wheel.

- You can undo changes you make to a document by using the Undo command. This command can be found on the Edit menu, or you can use the keyboard shortcut Ctrl+Z. You can redo changes you have undone by using the Redo command. Use Revert on the File menu to restore a document back to the state in which it was last saved.

- Use the Save command to save a document for the first time or after you make changes. If it is the first time a document has been saved, you'll be asked where to save the document and what to name the file. Documents are saved in the Expression Design native .design format. Use Save As to save a document under another name, or Save A Copy to save a copy of the document that leaves the original untouched.

Chapter at a Glance

Select objects,
page 48

Position objects,
page 61

Duplicate and
delete objects,
page 65

Transform objects,
page 66

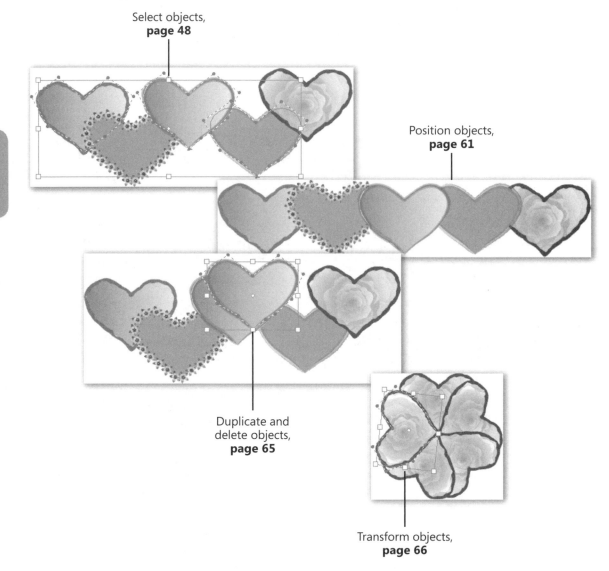

3 Manipulating Objects

In this chapter, you will learn to:

✔ Select objects.

✔ Group objects.

✔ Select anchor points.

✔ Position objects.

✔ Duplicate and delete objects.

✔ Transform objects.

One of the ways working with Microsoft Expression Design vector illustrations is different than working with photographs in programs such as Adobe Photoshop is that in Expression Design you can manipulate individual objects. As you learned in Chapter 1, "Working with Documents," you can manipulate vector objects without losing the quality or clarity of the images.

In this chapter, you will learn how to select specific objects, groups of objects, and even individual anchor points on objects. You will also learn how to move, duplicate, align, and delete objects, and how to transform them by scaling and rotating them.

Important Before you can use the practice files in this chapter, you need to install them from the book's companion CD to their default location. See "Using the Book's CD" at the beginning of this book for more information.

Troubleshooting Graphics and operating system–related instructions in this book reflect the Windows Vista user interface. If your computer is running Windows XP and you experience trouble following the instructions as written, please refer to the "Information for Readers Running Windows XP" section at the beginning of this book.

Selecting Objects

Selecting is one of the most important operations you can perform in Expression Design. When you *select* an object (or objects), that object is isolated, and you can make changes to the selected object without affecting the rest of the objects on the page. Various tools and menu items give you several ways to select the objects you need to edit.

Using the Selection Tool

The Selection tool is one of the most used (and useful) tools in Expression Design. With the Selection tool, you can change the display quality of an image and select or deselect single or multiple objects.

In this exercise, you will use the Selection tool to change the display quality of an image and practice manipulating objects.

USE the *objects.design* file. This practice file is located in the *Documents\Microsoft Press\ Expression Design SBS\ManipulatingObjects* folder.

BE SURE TO start Expression Design before beginning this exercise.

OPEN the *objects.design* file.

1. Verify that the *objects.design* file is displayed in Preview mode.

In this view, a large magenta rectangle appears in the middle of the page.

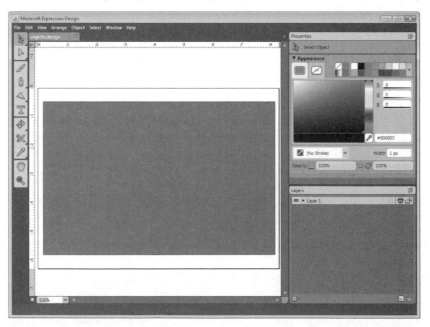

2. Press ⌈Ctrl⌉+⌈Y⌉, or click **Display Quality** on the **View** menu and then click **Wireframe**.

Wireframe view shows that there are five objects hidden behind the rectangle.

3. Press ⌈Ctrl⌉+⌈Y⌉ again, or click **Display Quality** on the **View** menu and then click **Preview**.

Only the magenta rectangle should be visible, just as it was following step 1.

4. In the **Toolbox**, click the **Selection** tool. Then, with the **Selection** tool, click the magenta rectangle once.

Selection

The rectangle is now selected. This means any editing you do will affect only the rectangle. Notice the eight hollow squares surrounding the rectangle. These *handles* are used for scaling, rotating, and skewing the selection. The dot indicates the center of the object.

> **Troubleshooting** If the handles are not displayed, point to Options on the Edit menu, click Display, select the Show Resize Handles check box, and then click OK.

Handles   Center point of selected object   Page border

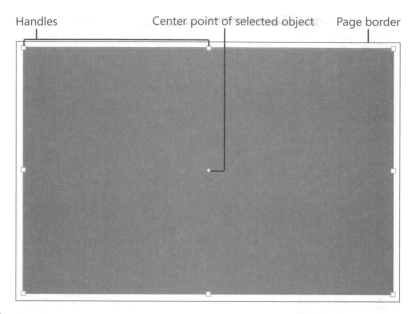

5. On the **Arrange** menu, point to **Order**, and then click **Send To Back**.

This sends the rectangle to the bottom of the stacking order, and the five shapes that were behind it become visible. Notice that the handles around the rectangle are still visible, showing that it is still selected. Also notice that the center dot is still visible.

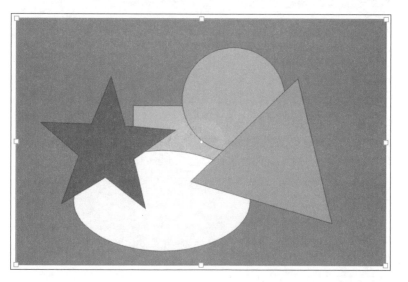

6. Click the blue star, and drag it on the page to move it.

7. Hold the [shift] key and click the yellow oval.

Both the blue star and yellow oval are now selected; multiple selected objects are treated as a single object. The handles surround both shapes, and the center dot is the center of the boundaries of both objects.

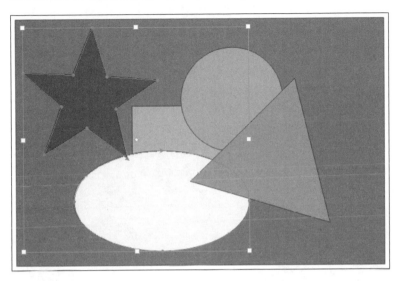

8. Drag the selected objects on the page. The objects move together as one.

9. Deselect the objects by clicking any empty area on the workspace or page; that is, an area that does not contain an object.

> **Tip** The easiest way to deselect all currently selected objects is to click away from them as you just did. If you prefer to use menus, click Deselect on the Select menu. If you prefer keyboard shortcuts, the deselect shortcut is Ctrl+Shift+A.

10. Place your pointer in the upper-left corner of the page, outside the magenta rectangle. Then drag down and to the right so that the pointer touches the star, and keep dragging so that it touches the green square.

This is called dragging a marquee. *Dragging a marquee* around objects to select them is often the fastest way to select multiple objects. You do not have to completely encircle them with the Selection tool's marquee; it is enough to just touch the object to add it to the selection.

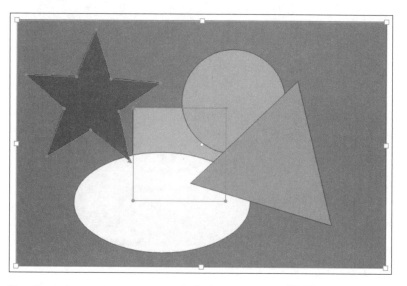

11. Deselect the magenta rectangle by pressing the ⟦Shift⟧ key and clicking the rectangle.

The blue star and green square are still selected, but the rectangle is no longer a part of the selection.

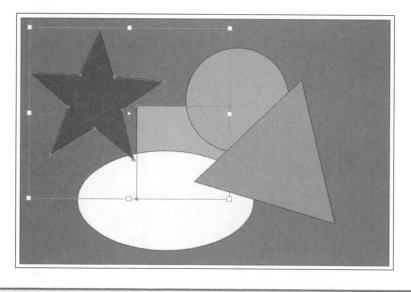

CLOSE the *objects.design* file without saving any changes.

Using the Select Menu

The Select menu has several commands that give you selection options beyond those available with the Selection tool. These include the following:

- **Select All** selects all of the unlocked objects on the page.

> **Tip** Objects can be locked to protect them from being accidentally edited, including being moved or transformed. Locked objects cannot be selected. To lock a selected object or objects, on the Arrange menu, click Lock. To unlock locked objects so they can be edited, on the Arrange menu, click Unlock All.

- **Deselect** deselects the currently selected object. The Deselect command is used to remove all selections at once. It works the same as the "click away" method we have been using.

- **Invert** selects the opposite of the current selection. (All of the objects that are currently selected will be deselected, and all of the objects that are not currently selected will be selected.)

- **Select By** allows you to select objects based on criteria you choose in the Select By dialog box.

In this exercise, you will use the options on the Select menu to select and deselect objects on the page, invert the selection, and select objects according to their attributes.

> **USE** the *hearts.design* file. This practice file is located in the *Documents\Microsoft Press\ Expression Design SBS\ManipulatingObjects* folder.
>
> **OPEN** the *hearts.design* file.

1. On the **Edit** menu, point to **Options**, and click **Units and Grids**.

2. In the **Options** dialog box, under **Units**, set **Document Units** to **pixels**, and then click **OK**.

   When you first open the practice document, nothing should be selected.

3. On the **Select** menu, click **Select All** to select all of the unlocked objects in the document.

   All of the hearts in the document are now selected.

4. Click **Deselect** on the **Select** menu to deselect all of the hearts.

5. Click the heart with the rose fill to select it. Then, on the **Arrange** menu, click **Lock**. Once again, on the **Select** menu, click **Select All**.

Locked objects, objects placed on locked layers, and guides are ignored by this command and are not selected. Notice that all of the hearts are selected except the one with the rose fill, because it is locked.

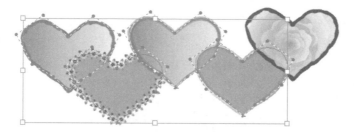

6. On the **Select** menu, click **Deselect** to deselect every object on the document.

7. On the **Arrange** menu, click **Unlock All** to unlock any locked objects.

In this case, there is only one, the rose-filled heart, which should now be selected. When you unlock all objects, any objects that were locked will be automatically selected.

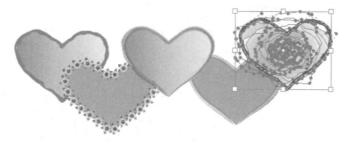

8. On the **Select** menu, click **Invert**.

The Invert command selects the opposite of what is currently selected. All objects that were not selected are now selected, and all objects that were selected are now deselected. Again, locked objects, objects on locked layers, and guides are ignored by this command. Because there were no locked objects and the rose-filled heart was the only object selected, inverting the selection selects the other four hearts on the page and deselects the rose-filled heart.

Selection

9. Use the **Selection** tool to select the rose-filled heart.

10. On the **Select** menu, click **Select By**.

The Select By dialog box opens.

Select By	✕
☑ Stroke name	
☐ Stroke color	
☐ Fill	
☐ Font	
OK	Cancel

The options in this dialog box let you quickly select objects based on their *attributes*. For example, you can select objects with a similar stroke or fill. The Select By dialog box contains check boxes for Stroke Name, Stroke Color, Fill, and Font.

11. Select the **Stroke name** check box, and then click **OK**.

The first and last hearts on the row are now selected because they use the same stroke. It doesn't matter if the strokes are the same color or width, as long as they use the same stroke name.

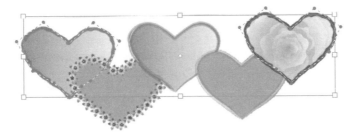

12. On the **Select** menu, click **Deselect**.

13. Click the pink gradient-filled heart in the middle to select it.

14. On the **Select** menu, click **Select By**.

15. In the **Select By** dialog box, select the **Fill** check box, and then click **OK**.

Both hearts with pink gradient fills are selected.

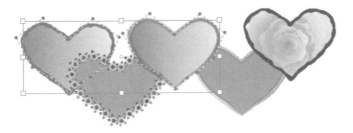

16. On the **Select** menu, click **Deselect**, and then click the pink gradient-filled heart in the middle to select it.

17. On the **Select** menu, click **Select By**.

18. In the **Select By** dialog box, select the **Stroke Color** check box, and then click **OK**.

    The three hearts with pink strokes are selected.

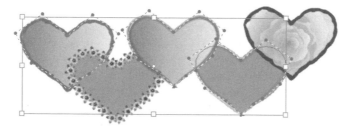

> **Tip** If no objects are selected on the page, Select By matches attributes of the object that is at the bottom of the stacking order. If no other objects on the page match the attributes of the bottom object, then nothing will be selected.

✕ **CLOSE** the *hearts.design* file without saving any changes.

Grouping Objects

When multiple objects are selected, they can be combined into a *group*. A group can be moved and manipulated as if it were one object. To create a group, you select the objects you want to include in the group, and then click Group on the Arrange menu. To disband, or *ungroup*, a group, click Ungroup on the Arrange menu.

A group differs from multiple selected objects. When you click an object in a multiple selection with the Selection tool, the object you click becomes selected, and the others are deselected. When you click any object in a group, you select the whole group.

In this exercise, you will group objects and manipulate an object group, use the Group Select tool to select one object in a group so it can be manipulated independently of the rest of the objects in the group, lock objects to protect them from being edited, and ungroup objects so they can be edited individually.

USE the *objects.design* file. This practice file is located in the *Documents\Microsoft Press\Expression Design SBS\ManipulatingObjects* folder.

OPEN the *objects.design* file.

1. Select the magenta rectangle. On the **Arrange** menu, click **Order**, and then click **Send To Back**.

   The rectangle moves behind the rest of the objects on the page.

2. Click the blue star, press and hold the [Shift] key, and click the green square. Then on the **Arrange** menu, click **Group**.

   One set of handles now surrounds both the blue star and green square, and these two shapes form a group. Dragging with the Selection tool moves the whole group.

   > **Tip** You can group selected objects by using the keyboard shortcut Ctrl+G.

Selection

Group Select

3. In the **Toolbox**, point to the **Selection** tool, and then click and hold down the mouse button to open the Selection tool's group.

4. In the tool group, click the **Group Select** tool to activate it.

5. Click away from the objects to deselect them.

6. Click the star or the square by using the **Group Select** tool.

   Only the object you click is selected.

7. Using the **Selection** tool, click the group of objects to select the whole group. You can now ungroup the objects by clicking **Ungroup** on the **Arrange** menu.

8. Click away from the objects to deselect all objects on the page.

9. Using the **Selection** tool, click the magenta rectangle to select it.

10. On the **Arrange** menu, click **Lock**.

    The rectangle is now locked and cannot be moved or edited.

    > **Tip** Locked objects do not display handles. When you lock an object or objects, you can work on other objects on the page without affecting the locked objects.

CLOSE the *objects.design* file without saving any changes.

Selecting Anchor Points

Not only can you select objects to edit, but you can also select specific anchor points so that they can be manipulated without affecting anything else on an object. Moving anchor points changes the shape of an object. With Expression Design drawing tools and its ability to precisely move individual anchor points, you can draw literally any shape. A simple example is editing letters in text to make one-of-a-kind lettering for a project, or moving anchor points to perfect a shape that needs a little tweaking.

> **Tip** Anchor points are also called *nodes*. These terms are interchangeable in Expression Design.

In this exercise, you will change the shape of an object by moving the anchor points.

USE the *objects.design* file. This practice file is located in the *Documents\Microsoft Press\ Expression Design SBS\ManipulatingObjects* folder.
OPEN the *objects.design* file.

1. Select the magenta rectangle. On the **Arrange** menu, click **Order**, and then click **Send To Back**.

   The rectangle moves behind the rest of the objects on the page.

Direct Selection

2. In the **Toolbox**, click the **Direct Selection** tool, and then click the star.

   The star is selected, but instead of handles, there are red dots at the corners.

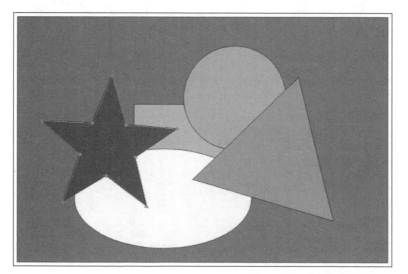

As discussed in Chapter 2, "Navigating the Workspace," these are the anchor *points*. All objects are created using vector paths, which have anchor points with line segments between them. These segments can be short or long, curved or straight, but they all have one very important feature in common: moving them changes the shape of the object.

See Also For more information about vector paths, see "Understanding the Difference Between Vector and Raster" in Chapter 1, "Working with Documents."

Zoom

3. If the anchor points are too small, use the **Zoom** tool to zoom in on the star.

4. Using the **Direct Selection** tool, click the top point of the star.

The selected anchor point remains red. The anchor points that are not selected have white edit handles. These look like the edit handles around an object selected with the Selection tool, but they are smaller.

Non-selected   Selected
anchor points   anchor point

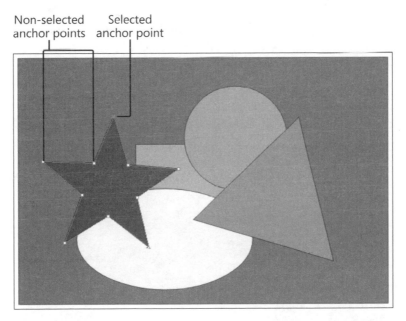

5. Using the **Direct Selection** tool, drag the selected anchor point to move it.

The shape of the star changes.

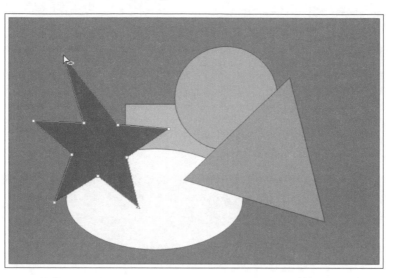

Clicking one of the white handles with the Direct Selection tool selects the anchor point and deselects the prior selection. Dragging moves the newly selected anchor point.

Lasso Selection

6. In the **Direct Selection** tool group, click the **Lasso Selection** tool.

7. Drag to select the two anchor points on the right side of the blue triangle. Then experiment with the handles to experience how moving different handles affects the points of the triangle.

Tip When an anchor point is selected, you can nudge it into precise position by using the Arrow keys. To move an anchor point one pixel at a time, press the Arrow key that points in the direction you want the anchor point to move, as many times as necessary to move it to the desired place on the page. To nudge an anchor point more than a pixel at a time, hold the Shift key as you press the Arrow key.

CLOSE the *objects.design* file without saving any changes.

The Lasso Selection Tool

The Lasso Selection tool has all the features of the Direct Selection tool, but offers more flexibility. If the anchor points are not displayed, you can click anywhere on the path with the Direct Selection or Lasso Selection tool to highlight the path and its anchor points. To select anchor points, use one of the three following techniques:

- Using the Direct Selection or the Lasso Selection tool, click an anchor point to select it.
- Using the Direct Selection tool, drag to select an area. Any anchor point that falls within the area you drag is selected.
- Using a circle or any irregular closed shape, drag to "lasso" all the anchor points that fall within the selection area. This is called *encircling*.

When you drag the Direct Selection or Lasso Selection tool to select an area that touches or crosses any other objects, you also select any anchor points on those objects in the selection area. To avoid selecting anchor points that you do not want selected, try locking those objects the same way you locked the rectangle in the previous exercise.

Positioning Objects

You have complete control over the position of objects on the page. You can move and align them in various ways, and distribute them evenly in any direction.

Tip Distributing objects is the act of spacing them evenly, either horizontally or vertically, on the page.

You've already moved objects by dragging them into position with the Selection tool, but there are other ways that allow for more precision, such as the following:

- You can use the Arrow keys to *nudge* an object into place.
- You can use the Action Bar for precise movement of any object or group of objects.

At times, you will want to position objects so that they line up. Or you might want to center them or space them evenly on the page. With the commands on the Align and Distribute menus, found on the Action Bar, you can perform these positioning operations with a few simple clicks.

> **Tip** To align or distribute objects, you must have more than one object selected to align and at least three to use the distribute command.

In this exercise, you will select and move objects by using the Arrow keys (← ↑ ↓ →), set options to control how objects respond to the use of the Arrow keys, and move objects precisely by using the Action Bar.

> **USE** the *hearts.design* file. This practice file is located in the *Documents\Microsoft Press\ Expression Design SBS\ManipulatingObjects* folder.
> **BE SURE TO** deselect any selected objects before beginning this exercise.
> **OPEN** the *hearts.design* file.

1. Select the pink heart on the left. Then press any Arrow key three times to nudge the heart three pixels in the direction of the arrow.

2. Hold the [Shift] key and press a different Arrow key to move the heart 10 pixels in the new key's direction.

> **Tip** The size of the movement can be set in the program options. To do so, point to Options on the Edit menu, and click Units And Grids. Then in the Options dialog box, with Units And Grids selected, change the Nudge Increment setting. The default is 1 pixel when the document units are set to pixels, and 1/10 of an inch when the document units are set to inches.

3. Hold the [Ctrl] key and press another Arrow key to move the heart 1/10 the nudge increment setting.

4. Select the center heart. Then, on the Action Bar, use the data entry boxes to change the x and/or y position of the heart. Either type coordinates into the data entry box or drag over the data entry box to change the values.

As you drag, the heart changes position on the page.

> **Tip** If you want to place an object in the center of the page, select it. On the Edit menu, click Cut. The object will be removed from the page and placed on the Windows clipboard. Then, on the Edit menu, click Paste, and the object will be pasted in the center of the page.

5. To align the hearts, first select all five by dragging a marquee around them.

6. On the **Action Bar**, display the **Align** menu.

You have several alignment choices on the Align menu; when working on your own, choose the one that suits your needs.

> **Tip** The same choices appear when you point to Align on the Arrange menu.

7. Click **Centers**.

All the hearts are stacked on top of each other in the center of the page.

8. Press Ctrl + Z to undo the change, and then on the **Align** menu, click **BottomEdges**.

The hearts all line up with their bottom edges even.

9. If the hearts are not selected, select them now. Then open the **Distribute** menu on the Action Bar.

Distribute ⌄
- Top Edges
- Bottom Edges
- Left Edges
- Right Edges
- Vertical Centers
- Horizontal Centers

> **Tip** The same choices appear when you point to Distribute on the Arrange menu.

10. Click **Horizontal Centers**.

All of the objects between the first and last objects move so that all the center points are evenly spaced horizontally.

The hearts can be evenly distributed across the page.

11. Click away from the hearts to deselect all objects. Then, using the **Selection** tool, click the last heart in the row to select it.

Selection

12. Press the → key repeatedly until the heart is at the right edge of the page.

> **Tip** Hold the Shift key as you press the Right Arrow key to move across the page faster.

13. Drag a marquee around all of the hearts to select them. Then, on the **Distribute** menu on the Action Bar, click **Horizontal Centers**.

The hearts are now distributed across the page.

14. Deselect by clicking away from the hearts. Then click the rightmost heart, point to **Order** on the **Arrange** menu, and click **Send Backward**.

15. Deselect by clicking away from the hearts.

CLOSE the *hearts.design* file without saving any changes.

Duplicating and Deleting Objects

You can duplicate a selected object or objects to create a copy. When you click Duplicate on the Edit menu, a copy of the selected object is placed slightly up and to the right of the original. To duplicate an object and place it in the center of the page, you can select it and click Copy on the Edit menu. The object is copied to the Windows clipboard, and clicking Paste on the Edit menu pastes the object in the center of the page.

If you want to place the duplicate in a specific place on the page, hold down the Alt key while dragging the object to the desired position. An easy way to create a duplicate is to press the Alt key either before or after you start to drag the original object. This creates a copy in the new location, as long you are holding the Alt key down when you release the mouse button.

You can easily delete objects you no longer need on the page. To delete, you can:

- Press the Delete key.
- Press the Backspace key.
- Click Delete on the Edit menu.
- Press Ctrl+X to cut the selection and place it on the clipboard so it can be pasted elsewhere on the page or into another document.

In this exercise, you will duplicate objects by using the Edit menu method and the drag method. You will also use the context menu to repeat the duplication, and you will delete objects you no longer need from the document.

> **USE** the *hearts.design* file. This practice file is located in the *Documents\Microsoft Press\ Expression Design SBS\ManipulatingObjects* folder.
>
> **OPEN** the *hearts.design* file.

1. Select the center heart, and on the **Edit** menu, click **Duplicate**.

   A copy of the object is placed slightly up and to the right of the original.

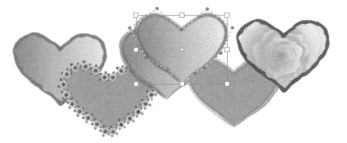

2. Select the left heart, and press and hold the [Alt] key as you drag the selected heart.

   When you release the mouse button, a copy of the object is placed in the mouse position. This is called dragging a duplicate and is a quick way to duplicate an object or group of objects and position them on the page at the same time.

3. Select and then right-click the right heart. On the shortcut menu, click **Transform**, and then click **Repeat Last Transform**.

4. To delete the heart you just duplicated, click the heart if necessary to select it, and then click **Delete** on the **Edit** menu.

5. To delete the two other duplicate hearts, select them both, and then press [Del] on your keyboard.

> **CLOSE** the *hearts.design* file without saving any changes.

Transforming Objects

You can easily transform an object in several ways by clicking and using the edit handles to drag the object.

By dragging the edit handles, you can scale objects larger or smaller in the following ways:

● Dragging a corner handle inward makes the object smaller.

● Dragging a corner handle outward makes the object larger.

- Holding Shift as you drag inward or outward scales the object, retaining the width and height proportions.

- Holding Alt as you drag inward or outward scales the object from the center. This is handy when you do not want to move the object on the page, but only want to change its size.

- Holding Shift and Alt as you drag inward or outward scales the object from the center, retaining the width and height proportions.

- Dragging a center top or bottom handle inward or outward changes the height of an object.

- Dragging a center side handle inward or outward changes the width of an object.

- Holding Shift and dragging any center handle inward or outward scales the object while retaining the height and width proportions.

- Holding Shift and Alt as you drag any center handle inward or outward retains the height and width proportions while scaling from the center.

You can rotate objects by using the corner edit handles. When you point to any corner handle, the mouse pointer turns into a rotate pointer. With the rotate pointer, you can:

- Click and drag to rotate the object.

- Hold Alt as you rotate to duplicate the object.

- Hold Shift as you rotate to constrain the rotation to a 45-degree or 90-degree angle.

> **Tip** You can change the angle of the rotation increment in the Options dialog box. To do so, click Options on the Edit menu and point to Units And Grids. Under Arrangement, change the number of rotation steps. The default is 8, which will constrain the increments to 45-degree angles (which is 360 degrees divided by 8). To set a custom setting, divide 360 degrees by the angle to which you want to constrain, and enter the resulting number in the rotation steps box.

> **Tip** Using the *Registration button* in the Action Bar, you can change the *reference point* of an object. The reference point is the point that remains stationary while the rest of the object scales or rotates around it.

Transformations can be repeated. A nice feature in Expression Design is the ability to duplicate a transformation. This is useful when you want to make objects follow around a circle, for instance.

In this exercise, you will copy and paste an object from one document into a new document you create from scratch, and you will save the file by using Save As. You will also scale and rotate objects by using the transform handles and the Action Bar, repeat a transformation, and revert to the last saved version of the file, discarding all changes.

> **USE** the *hearts.design* file. This practice file is located in the *Documents\Microsoft Press\ Expression Design SBS\ManipulatingObjects* folder.
> **OPEN** the *hearts.design* file.

1. Select any one of the hearts on the page. Then on the **Edit** menu, click **Copy**.

2. On the **File** menu, click **New**.

   The New Document dialog box opens.

3. In the **New Document** dialog box, click **OK** to accept the default settings and create a new document.

4. With the new document active, on the **Edit** menu, click **Paste** to place the copied heart onto the page.

5. On the **File** menu, click **Save**.

   The Save As dialog box opens.

6. In the **Save As** dialog box, name the file **transform**, and then click **OK**.

7. To scale the heart by using the edit handles, select the heart and then point to a corner handle until the resize pointer appears.

Scale

8. Drag outward to scale the heart larger or inward to scale it smaller.

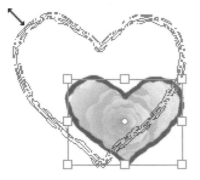

9. Release the mouse button to commit the transformation.

10. With the heart still selected, in the Action Bar, drag across the **Width** box to increase the size of the heart.

The chain link between the Width and Height boxes indicates that the width and height of the selected object are linked. This means that if you change the width, the height will change proportionally, and vice versa. Or, to put it another way, the object will be scaled at a 1:1 ratio.

> **Tip** If you want to change the width of an object without changing the height (and vice versa), click the chain to break the link.

Rotate

11. To rotate the heart by using the edit handles, point outside a corner handle until the rotate pointer is displayed.

12. Drag to rotate the object.

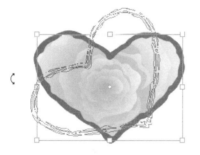

13. Hold the [Shift] key and drag, to rotate the heart in 45-degree increments.

14. Release the mouse button to commit the transformation.

15. With the heart still selected, in the Action Bar, drag in the **Rotation Angle** box.

16. Release the mouse button to commit the rotation.

17. On the **File** menu, click **Revert**. When asked if you want to revert to the last saved version, click **Yes**.

> **Tip** Press F12 to quickly revert an image back to the last saved state.

Registration
Point

18. To rotate around a specific point, select the reference point by clicking the **Registration Point** button on the left side of the Action Bar.

19. Click one of the squares on the **Registration Point** button to correspond with the point on the object around which you want it to pivot. This is called the reference point.

Clicking the bottom-center point on the Registration Point button pivots the heart around that anchor point. To rotate the heart, point the mouse just outside any corner handle, and then drag when the rotate pointer appears.

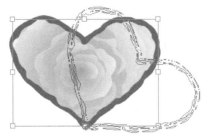

20. To repeat the last transformation, on the **Arrange** menu, point to **Transform**, and then click **Repeat Last Transform**.

The heart rotates again with the same angle increment as before.

> **Tip** It is much easier to repeat the last transformation by using the keyboard shortcut Ctrl+D.

21. On the **File** menu, click **Revert**. As before, click **Yes** when asked if you want to revert to the last saved version of the file.

22. Set the reference point to the bottom point of the heart, and then point outside a corner handle until the rotate pointer is displayed.

23. Start dragging to rotate the heart, and then hold the [Alt] key to duplicate as you rotate.

24. Release the mouse button when the second heart is in the position you want.

You now have two hearts, at two different angles.

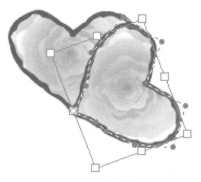

25. Without doing anything else, immediately press [Ctrl]+[D] three times to repeat the rotation and duplication.

This repeat duplication makes it very easy to quickly make a flower.

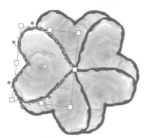

CLOSE the *transform.design* file, saving your changes. If you are not continuing directly on to the next chapter, exit Expression Design.

Key Points

- Selecting is one of the most important operations you can perform in Expression Design.
- You must select an object to make changes to it.
- Group two or more separate objects to treat them as a unit.
- Expression Design offers many tools with which you can select objects, groups, and individual anchor points.
- The Select menu offers some unique ways to select objects, such as selecting by attributes.
- You can rotate, scale, and perform other transformations by using either the Action Bar or the edit handles on the object.
- You can use the Action Bar for precise movement, scaling, and transformations.
- You can duplicate objects by holding Alt as you drag, by using the context menu, or by clicking Duplicate on the Object menu.
- You can repeat transformations by using the Ctrl+D keyboard shortcut.
- You can transform and create a duplicate at the same time by holding down the Alt key as you transform.
- You can delete selected objects by pressing Delete or Backspace, or by clicking Delete on the Edit menu.
- You can copy selected objects to the clipboard so they can be pasted into another position or another document.

Chapter at a Glance

Understand layers,
page 74

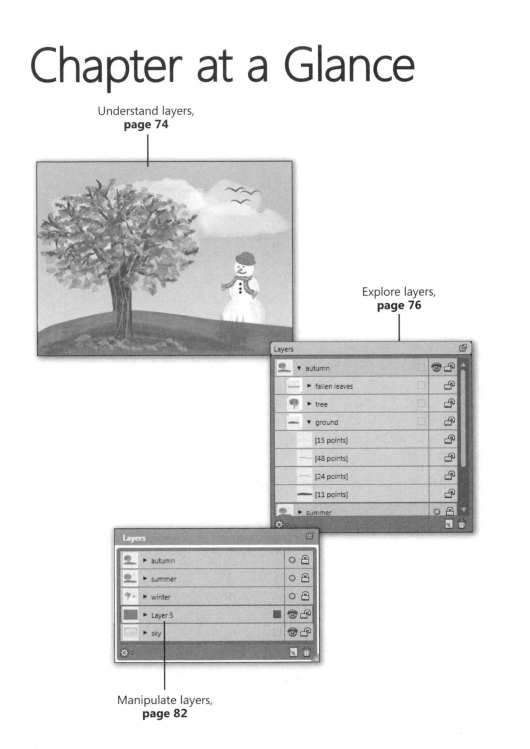

Explore layers,
page 76

Manipulate layers,
page 82

4 Working with Layers

In this chapter, you will learn to:

✔ Understand layers.

✔ Explore layers.

✔ Manipulate layers.

✔ Set layer options.

One of the best features of Microsoft Expression Design is its use of layers. Layers give you the flexibility to design several versions of a document, decide what parts of a document will be printable, and much more.

In this chapter, you will first learn what layers are and why they are important. You will learn how to use the Layers panel to expand, collapse, add, delete, move, hide, and group layers. You will also learn to use the Layers panel to select groups of objects in one step.

Important Before you can use the practice files in this chapter, you need to install them from the book's companion CD to their default location. See "Using the Book's CD" at the beginning of this book for more information.

Troubleshooting Graphics and operating system–related instructions in this book reflect the Windows Vista user interface. If your computer is running Windows XP and you experience trouble following the instructions as written, please refer to the "Information for Readers Running Windows XP" section at the beginning of this book.

Understanding Layers: What They Are and Why They Are Important

The *layers* concept is one that is often very difficult for new users of graphics software to grasp. The truth is, once you understand the concept, you will be amazed that you were ever able to work without them. To cite one simple example, when you put an object on another layer, you can show or hide the object or make it non-printing.

Using layers, you can easily hide and show whole layouts. One use for this technique is to create a two-sided document, such as a brochure or greeting card, and put all content for the front on one layer, and all content for the back on another layer. By showing one layer and hiding the other, you can work on (or print) the front or back independently, yet both layers are conveniently saved in one document.

So what exactly are layers?

In Expression Design, layers are like virtual stacks of transparent pages. These stacks function like the transparent plastic pages in some biology textbook illustrations. For instance, imagine an illustration of a hand, showing the skin. When you turn the skin page, an image of the muscles, blood vessels, and bone appears underneath. Flip the next page and the muscle page is transparent, showing the vessels and bone beneath, and so on. Layers are like those transparent pages: transparent areas of the layer let the lower layers remain visible. The areas on the layer that contain *content* hide whatever is on the layers below.

Layers are accessible from the Layers panel. From this panel, layers can be manipulated, hidden, moved, grouped, and much more.

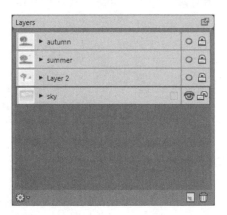

In the Layers panel, layers are shown in the layers list. Layers are displayed in the Layers panel in the order in which their content is on the page; the top layer is at the top of the stacking order. Each layer has a small thumbnail of the layer content to the left of its name.

In this exercise, you will explore the Layers panel and the layers in a file. You will float the Layers panel in the workspace, and then display a magnified thumbnail view of the layer's contents.

> **USE** the *layers.design* file. This practice file is located in the *Documents\Microsoft Press\ Expression Design SBS\UnderstandingLayers* folder.
>
> **BE SURE TO** start Expression Design before beginning this exercise.

1. Open the *layers.design* file.

In the image window, you should see blue sky and clouds. In the right pane of the workspace in the Layers panel, the layer thumbnail shows a small representation of the layer contents, in this case the blue sky and clouds.

2. Click the **Float** button to float the panel in the workspace.

Float

You can now drag the panel in the workspace and place it where it is convenient. Whether you choose to float the panel or leave it docked in the pane is a matter of personal preference.

> **Tip** If the Layers panel is not visible, click Layers on the Window menu to open it.

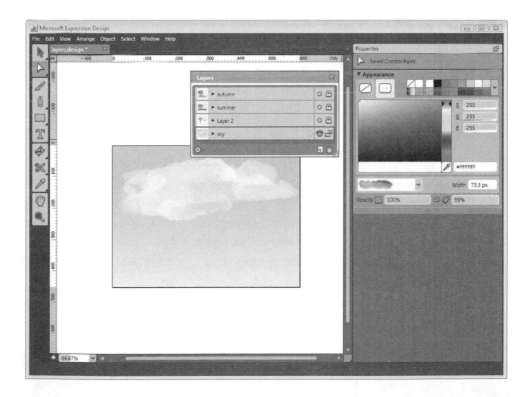

This image has four layers: *sky*, *Layer 2*, *summer*, and *autumn*. *Sky* is the bottom layer in the Layers panel, making it the bottom layer in the stacking order. When the layers are visible, the content in the *Layer 2*, *summer*, and *autumn* layers will show above the *sky* layer.

3. Point to the **summer** thumbnail.

A larger pop-up thumbnail appears, showing the contents of the layer.

> **Tip** If the thumbnail does not pop up when you point to it, click the Layer Options button. Then, on the Layer Options menu, click Thumbnail Options, and click Popup Thumbnails. Note that you can also set the size of the layer thumbnail here. You can choose from Large, Medium, or Small, or you can turn layer thumbnails off altogether by choosing None.

Exploring Layers

With the Layers panel, you have a lot of control over many aspects of your document. You can show and hide layers, add new layers, delete layers you no longer need, or rename the layers. You can also select a whole layer or specific objects on a layer so that you can easily group layers or to change the stacking order.

Naming, Hiding, and Collapsing and Expanding Layers

A single document can have many layers, each with different properties and content. Every Expression Design document always contains at least one layer. When you create a new document, Expression Design automatically creates an empty layer. By default, this layer is named *Layer 1*. When you add new layers, they are named consecutively: *Layer 2*, *Layer 3*, and so on. However, it is very helpful, especially in a document with many layers, to name the layers with meaningful names.

A button on the right side of the Layers panel shows whether each layer is hidden or visible. When a layer is hidden, the button looks like a circle, and when a layer is visible, the button looks like an eyeball. For example, in the *layers.design* file, the *sky* layer displays the eyeball; the other three layers display the circle because they are hidden.

Because Expression Design is a vector drawing program, most of its files have hundreds of objects. Each brush stroke you lay down, every shape you draw, every object added to the page is a separate object with its own sub-layer in the Layers panel. An image with many layers can make the Layers panel very long and hard to navigate. You can keep the panel manageable by collapsing and expanding it when you need to access an object on the layer. When layers are expanded, the object lists for each layer are visible, including groups.

In this exercise, you will name layers in the Layers panel. Then you will hide and show layer content in the image window by using the Toggle Layer Visibility button in the Layers panel. You will also keep the size of the Layers panel manageable by collapsing and expanding layers.

> **USE** the *layers.design* file. This practice file is located in the *Documents\Microsoft Press\ Expression Design SBS\UnderstandingLayers* folder.
>
> **OPEN** the *layers.design* file, if it is not already open.

1. In the **Layers** panel, double-click **Layer 2**, and replace the text with the word **winter**.

2. Press [Enter] to commit the change. Click **Save** on the **File** menu to save the changes to the file.

Layers		
▶ autumn	○	🔒
▶ summer	○	🔒
▶ winter	○	🔒
▶ sky		👁 🔓

Visibility On

Visibility Off

3. On the **sky** layer, click the **Toggle Layer Visibility** button.

The image window is now blank because the *sky* layer is hidden.

4. Click the **Toggle Layer Visibility** button to make the **sky** layer visible again.

5. On the **winter** layer, click the **Toggle Layer Visibility** button to make it visible.

Layers		
▶ autumn	○	🔒 —— Hidden layer
▶ summer	○	🔒
▶ winter		👁 🔓 —— Visible layer
▶ sky		👁 🔓

The image window now displays snow on the ground, a snowman, and a tree with bare branches from the *winter* layer, and sky and clouds from the *sky* layer. The area around the objects in the winter layer is transparent, allowing the objects in the sky layer to show through.

6. On the **sky** layer, click the **Toggle Layer Visibility** button.

The sky and clouds disappear from the image window.

7. On the **sky** layer, click the **Toggle Layer Visibility** button to redisplay the layer.

8. On the **summer** layer, click the **Toggle Layer Visibility** button.

The image window displays a green summer tree, some birds, and a patch of green grass. The rest of the *summer* layer is transparent. Because of the transparency, the sky and clouds from the *sky* layer and the snowman from the *winter* layer are also visible.

> **Tip** You can toggle the visibility of all the layers except one by pressing Alt and clicking on the Toggle Layer Visibility button of the layer you want to keep visible.

Expand

9. In the **Layers** panel, in the list of layers, click the **Expand** button on the **autumn** layer to display the object list.

The layer expands to show the object list for the layer, which consists of three groups: *fallen leaves*, *tree*, and *ground*. All three groups in this layer are collapsed.

10. Click the **Expand** button to the left of the ground group to expand the group and display its object list.

Layers	
▼ autumn	
► fallen leaves	
► tree	
▼ ground	
[15 points]	
[48 points]	
[24 points]	
[11 points]	
► summer	

11. On the **autumn** layer, click the **Collapse** button to close the object list.

Collapse

> ✕ **BE SURE TO** collapse all of the layers in the Layers panel before continuing to the next exercise.

> **Tip** As you add paths and objects to a document, Expression Design gives them generic names, such as *[5 points]*. Consider naming important paths, groups, or objects to find them quickly if you want to select them to be edited or moved to another layer.

Selecting, Locking, and Grouping Layers

Layers cannot be selected if they are not visible, nor can they be selected if they are locked. When a layer is visible, a hollow square button displays to the right of the name. This button is used to select all unlocked content on a layer.

You can lock and unlock layers by using the Toggle Lock buttons in the Layers panel. These buttons have two states, *locked* and *unlocked*, as indicated by the corresponding padlock images. Locking a layer works the same as locking an object, with the exception that when you lock a layer, the entire layer is locked and none of the objects on it can be edited or moved. When you lock a layer, it is protected from being changed by the accidental move of an object on the page. It is also protected from global changes you make to the rest of the document.

Hidden layers are always locked; unlocking a layer makes it visible. You can lock a visible layer, too, so that the objects on the locked layer are still visible but you cannot accidentally move, delete, or alter the objects on it.

Grouping similar objects and/or paths together often makes them much easier to work with. However, objects and paths can be difficult to select when there are many of them or they are behind other objects. To make this task easier, you can expand a layer in the Layers panel so the object list is displayed, and then press Shift while clicking the objects you want to select. You can then group the objects by clicking Group on the Arrange menu. To ungroup grouped objects, click Ungroup on the Arrange menu. Groups can be contained within each other.

Grouping objects by using the Layers panel is often easier than selecting objects by clicking on them, because an object that is behind another can be difficult to select. Selecting via the Layers panel is also easier when you have many objects to select at once, as you will understand when you try to select all of the branches or leaves at once.

In the following exercise, you will select layers and lock and unlock them by using the Layers panel. You will also group objects in the Layers panel to organize them and make difficult selections easier.

> **USE** the *layers.design* file. This practice file is located in the *Documents\Microsoft Press\ Expression Design SBS\UnderstandingLayers* folder.
>
> **OPEN** the *layers.design* file, if it is not already open.

Visibility Off

Layer Selection

1. Click the **summer** layer's **Toggle Layer Visibility** button.

The *sky* layer should be visible, and the *autumn* and *winter* layers hidden.

2. Click the **Layer Selection** button on the **summer** layer to select all content on the layer.

Because there are no locked objects, all layer content will be selected. The square button turns solid blue, and you will be able to see the paths on all objects on the layer in the image window. In this case, the summer tree, leaves on the ground, and the birds are selected.

> **Tip** When an object is low in the stacking order, it can be hard to select with the selection tools. If you click the object's thumbnail or name in the Layers panel, you can easily select it.

3. Click the **Toggle Layer Visibility** button on the **autumn** and **winter** layers.

Notice that the *autumn* and *winter* layers are locked and therefore cannot be selected. The *summer* layer is unlocked and selected; the *sky* layer is unlocked and not selected. Because the *sky* layer is not locked, if you click the clouds or the sky background in the image, they would become selected, along with their layer.

> **Tip** You can hold the Alt key as you click a Lock button to lock all layers except the layer you clicked. If all of the other layers are currently locked, holding Alt as you click a Lock button unlocks them all.

4. Experiment with locking and unlocking layers to get a feel for how the feature works by clicking the Toggle Lock button for each of the layers.

5. Before continuing, click **Revert** on the **File** menu to return the file to the state from which it was last saved.

   This should leave the file in the same state it was in when you started this exercise.

Visibility Off

6. Show the **summer** layer by clicking its **Toggle Layer Visibility** button.

7. In the **Layers** panel, expand the **summer** layer by clicking the **Expand** button.

Expand

8. Expand the tree group by clicking its **Expand** button.

   The *tree* group has three groups within it: *leaves*, *branches*, and *trunk*. The branches would be extremely difficult to select without the Layers panel, because many of them are behind leaves, but it is a simple matter to select all of them from the object list.

Layers
▼ tree
► leaves
► branches
► trunk
► grass
► ground
► Layer 2
► sky

9. In the **tree** group, select **branches**, and then on the **Arrange** menu, click **Group**.

   The leaves would be hard to select for the sheer number of them and the fact that they are intermingled with the small upper branches of the tree. Selecting groups of items from the object list greatly simplifies this task.

> **BE SURE TO** click Revert on the File menu to return the document to the last saved state before continuing.

Manipulating Layers

Layers are even more useful in that you can arrange them to suit your purposes. Add them to your document window, delete them, reorder them, or move objects from one layer to another, all by way of simple, intuitive controls.

Adding a New Layer

As you work in Expression Design, you will very often want to add new layers to your documents. Objects on their own layers are easy to hide and show, so you can try different versions of an illustration while retaining the original version, all within one file. In the *layers.design* file, a new layer was used to add autumn leaves on the tree while retaining the green summer leaves.

Layers also give you the flexibility to print only part of the design. One way this technique can be used is to design the front and back of a greeting card on separate layers. The back layer can be hidden so the front layer can be edited or printed, or you can hide the front layer to print or edit on the back.

In this exercise, you will add a new layer to the document.

USE the *layers.design* file. This practice file is located in the *Documents\Microsoft Press\ Expression Design SBS\UnderstandingLayers* folder.

OPEN the *layers.design* file, if it is not already open.

1. In the **Layers** panel, click the **sky** layer to select it.

   This can also be referred to as making it the active layer.

New Layer

2. To add a new layer to the document, click the **New Layer** button at the bottom of the **Layers** panel.

   A new layer called *Layer 5* displays directly above the *sky* layer.

3. Select the **Rectangle** tool, and drag a rectangle of any size in the image window. The rectangle displays on *Layer 5*, above the *sky* layer.

> **Note** Stroke and Fill are not important as long as something is added to *Layer 5*.

4. Keep the image open so it can be used in the next exercise.

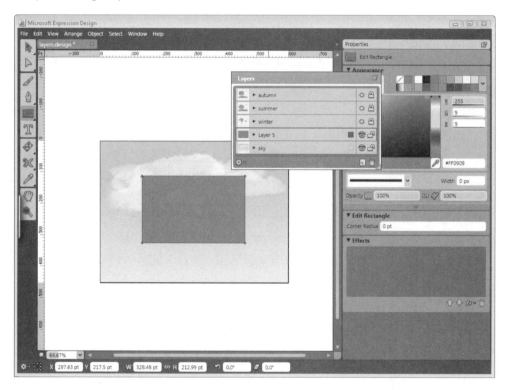

> **Tip** By default, Expression Design adds the new layer immediately above the layer that is currently selected. If you prefer the new layer to be added to the beginning of the layer list, so that the layer goes immediately to the top of the stacking order, point to Options on the Edit menu, and then click General to open the General options page. Clear the Create New Layer Above Current Layer check box, and then click OK to accept the change.

Deleting Layers and Changing Layer Order

Not only can you create layers, you can delete them as well. The beauty of layers is that they give you the freedom to make many changes to an image without changing the original. After you decide on the final design, you can easily delete any unnecessary layers.

You can also change the stacking order of layers. To move layers up or down in the stacking order, drag and drop them into place in the Layers panel.

In this exercise, you will delete layers and change their stacking order by using the Layers panel.

> **USE** the *layers.design* file. This practice file is located in the *Documents\Microsoft Press\ Expression Design SBS\UnderstandingLayers* folder.
>
> **OPEN** the *layers.design* file, if it is not already open.

Trash

1. Select **Layer 5**, and then in the lower portion of the **Layers** panel, click the **Trash** button to delete the layer.

Trash button

The Delete Layer dialog box opens.

2. In the **Delete Layer** dialog box, click **Yes** to confirm the deletion.

3. In the **Layers** panel, drag the **winter** layer to position it above the **summer** layer and below the **autumn** layer.

4. When the yellow line displays, drop the layer into place.

The stacking order of the layers changes.

Moving Objects to Another Layer

Often, to keep similar or related objects together, you might want to move them to another layer. You can do this by using the Layers panel. Whenever you create a new object, Expression Design's default action is to place it on the layer that is currently selected in the Layers panel. When you select any object on the page, the Layers panel automatically selects the layer the object is on, as long as the layer is unlocked. To move a selected object from one layer to another, expand the source layer in the Layers panel so that the object list is visible. Drag the object to another position on the same layer, or to another layer. When the yellow line displays under the name, drop the object.

An object can be copied to another layer by using the Copy command to copy it from one layer and the Paste command to paste it to another. This places a copy of the object on the new layer while leaving the original on the layer from which it was copied. To remove the object from one layer and place it on another, use the Cut command.

In this exercise, you will move objects to another layer by dragging and dropping in the Layers panel and by using the Copy and Cut commands.

> **USE** the *layers.design* file. This practice file is located in the *Documents\Microsoft Press\ Expression Design SBS\UnderstandingLayers* folder.
>
> **OPEN** the *layers.design* file, if it is not already open.

1. Make sure the **summer** layer is visible. Expand the **summer** layer, and select the **tree** group.

2. Expand the **sky** layer. If you cannot see all of the layers, resize the panel by pulling down and dragging the bottom-right corner.

3. Drag the **tree** group to the **sky** layer, and drop it under the **clouds** group when the yellow line is visible.

The *tree* group is now on the *sky* layer, between the *sky* object and the *clouds* group, and the *tree* group should be selected.

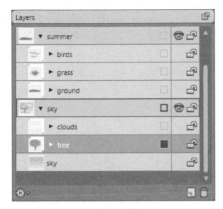

> **Tip** If you drag an object to the layer rather than to a position in the object list of that layer, it is placed at the bottom of the stacking order in the new layer.

4. Click **Cut** on the **Edit** menu. Select the **summer** layer. Click **Paste** on the **Edit** menu, and the **tree** group will be moved from the **sky** layer to the **summer** layer.

   Using the Cut command removes objects from the layer and places them on the layer you paste them onto.

5. Collapse the **summer** layer. Click the **Toggle Layer Visibility** button to display the **winter** layer, and then expand the layer. Select the **derby** group.

6. On the **Edit** menu, click **Copy**.

7. Select the **sky** layer, then click **Paste** on the **Edit** menu to paste the **derby** group onto the **sky** layer.

8. Click the **Toggle Layer Visibility** buttons on the **summer** and **winter** layers to hide them.

   The derby graphic should be visible in the image window, and if you look at the *sky* layer in the layers panel, the *derby* group is now above the *clouds* group.

> **Tip** When you paste using the Copy command, the selection is placed in the center of the page. To copy the selection to the top of the stack, on the Edit menu, click Paste In Front. The selection is copied to the new layer in the same position on the page it occupied on the original layer at the top of the stack. To copy the selection to the bottom of the stack, on the Edit menu, click Paste In Back and it will be pasted in the same position on the page, but at the bottom of the stack. This is true when pasting to the same layer or to another layer.

9. Experiment with these options in the practice file, moving any of the groups to another layer, cutting, copying, and trying the **Paste In Front** and **Paste In Back** commands from the previous tip. Make sure the layer you want to copy or move to is visible and not locked.

> **Tip** Although it would seem to be exactly what you want, the Paste With Layer command on the Edit menu will not move the selection to another layer. It places the object back on the original layer.

CLOSE the *layers.design* file without saving your changes. If you are not continuing directly to the next chapter, exit Expression Design.

Setting Layer Options

At the bottom of the Layers panel is the Layer Options button, which opens the Layer Options menu. On this menu are several options you should be aware of:

- **New Layer.** Use this option to create a new layer above the current layer.
- **Duplicate Layer.** Use this to create a copy of the layer above the original with *copy* appended to its name.
- **Delete Layer.** Use this option to throw the selected layer in the Trash.
- **Layer Color.** Use this option to show the color paths when objects are selected on the layer.
- **Layer Render Style.** Use this sub-menu to access the same options that are available in **Display Quality** on the **View** menu, with the addition of Path. (See Chapter 2, "Navigating the Workspace.")
- **Thumbnail Options.** Use this sub-menu to control the display of thumbnails, as discussed in "Understanding Layers" earlier in this chapter.

Key Points

- Layers are like stacks of transparent paper. Where there is content, the layer is opaque; where there is no content, the layer is transparent, letting objects on the layers below show through.

- You can rename layers in the Layers panel by double-clicking the layer's name and typing a new name. Press Enter to commit the change.

- You can use the Toggle Layer Visibility button to show and hide layer content. Hold the Alt key as you click the button to toggle visibility for all other layers at once.

- Hidden layers are always locked and cannot be selected. You can lock or unlock visible layers.

- You can select a layer's contents by clicking its square layer selection button. Remember, you cannot select a locked layer.

- You can expand and collapse object lists in the Layers panel to make the panel easier to scroll through.

- You can lock layers to protect them from accidental movements or object deletions and to protect them against global changes made to the document.

- You can select hard-to-reach objects by clicking them in the Layers panel object list. You can then group or ungroup them by clicking the corresponding command on the Arrange menu.

- You can add new layers by clicking the New Layer button at the bottom of the Layers panel. By default, new layers are added above the currently selected layer.

- You can easily delete layers you no longer need by selecting them and clicking the Trash button at the bottom of the Layers panel.

- You can change the stacking order of layers by dragging them in the Layers panel to a new position.

- You can use the Layer Options menu at the bottom of the Layers panel to create, duplicate, and delete layers or set options for layers.

Chapter at a Glance

Explore path anatomy, **page 92**

Use the shape and line tools, **page 94**

Create and edit cusp points, **page 111**

Modify paths with path operations, **page 117**

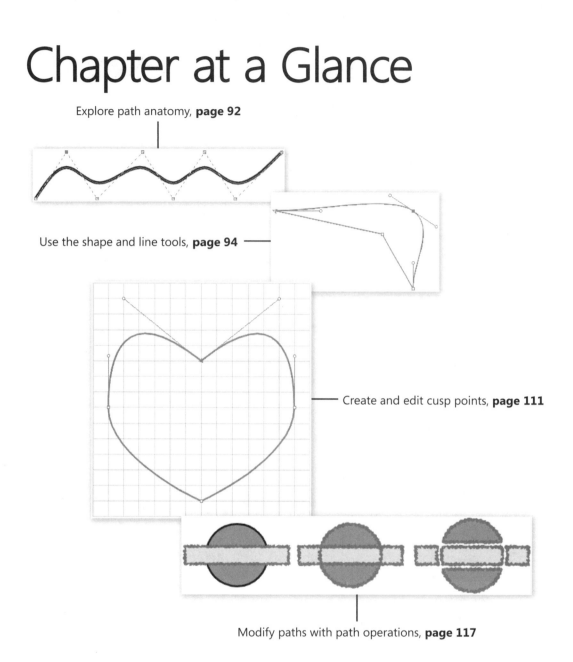

5 Using the Drawing Tools

In this chapter, you will learn to:

- ✔ Explore path anatomy.
- ✔ Use the shape and line tools.
- ✔ Use the page grid.
- ✔ Use the Pen tool.
- ✔ Use the B-Spline tool.
- ✔ Create and edit cusp points.
- ✔ Make compound paths.
- ✔ Modify paths with path operations and clipping.

In this chapter, you will learn to use the Microsoft Expression Design shape and drawing tools. You can combine these tools to draw whatever you want. You will also be introduced to Bézier and B-Spline curves, and learn to control the curves by using practice templates. Predicting where the lines will fall when you are using the Pen and *B-Spline tools* is one of the most important parts of using them, and it is also the most confusing. This chapter will give you some hands-on practice to make the logic of their usage easier to grasp.

When it comes to placement with the grids in Expression Design, you can place objects on the page with accuracy.

Important Before you can use the practice files in this chapter, you need to install them from the book's companion CD to their default location. See "Using the Book's CD" at the beginning of this book for more information.

Troubleshooting Graphics and operating system–related instructions in this book reflect the Windows Vista user interface. If your computer is running Windows XP and you experience trouble following the instructions as written, please refer to the "Information for Readers Running Windows XP" section at the beginning of this book.

Exploring Path Anatomy

A path is the fundamental element of vector graphics, just as the pixel is the fundamental element of raster graphics. But although a pixel is nothing more than a very small, colored square, a path is a mathematical description. It's like a set of instructions that tells your computer how to draw whatever it is that you want to depict. A pixel by itself is not terribly useful; you need to arrange hundreds or thousands of them into a grid before you can resolve an image. But a path is complete unto itself. Although most vector graphics are composed of many paths working together, you can easily create a meaningful image—a line, a circle, a square—from one path.

Paths have a direction; that is to say, they have a start point and an endpoint. Paths can also be open or closed. An open path, such as a straight line, has a different start point and endpoint. A closed path, such as a square, has the same start point and endpoint. More on this a bit later.

Another curious difference between raster and vector graphics is that pixels are always called pixels, whereas paths go by many names. Throughout this book, we use terms such as *curves*, *shapes*, *outlines*, *vector objects*, and *paths* interchangeably.

When you use the drawing tools in Expression Design, you create paths. Expression Design supports two kinds: **Bézier curves** and **B-Spline curves**. A Bézier curve is a line or path composed of *segments* connected by anchor points (also known as *nodes*). Because Bézier curves are defined by mathematical equations, the vector files that contain them are typically smaller in size than raster files, and the drawings can be resized without any loss in quality.

The Father of Modern Computer Drawing

Pierre Bézier (1910-1999) was a French mathematician and engineer who developed a method of computer drawing in the late 1960s, consisting of straight or curved line segments connected by anchor points. Curve anchor points have control handles that are used to control the direction and shape of the segments. His contribution to computer graphics made much of the work we do in vector programs today possible. The objects made with the method he developed for computer drawing bear his name: Bézier curves.

Bézier curves have **control handles** that you use to alter the curves, both by moving them to change the angle and thus the direction of the curve, and by changing their length to change the depth of the curve. The longer the handle is, the deeper the curve will be.

Expression Design also lets your draw another kind of curve called a B-Spline Curve. B-Spline curves also are defined by anchor points and segments, but the anchor points usually lie off the path.

There are several types of paths. When the **endpoints** of a path are joined, you have a **closed path**. Circles and rectangles are closed paths, but a closed path can also be a freeform shape or object. The apple shown here is composed of three closed shapes: the apple, the stem, and the leaf.

An *open path* has endpoints that are not joined. Lines and arcs are examples of open paths. Open paths can be curved or straight or a combination of both.

Anchor points can be corner points or curve points. The type of point determines how the path segment will be affected when these points are manipulated. In the image shown here, one of the curve points is selected so that the control handles are displayed.

> **Tip** One anchor point is always an arrow to indicate the direction of the path. To change the direction of the path, select Reverse Path from the Object menu. When you stroke a path with a brush stroke, the stroke is applied in the direction of the arrow. If your stroke seems to be going the wrong way, reverse the path.

Using the Shape and Line Tools

One of the easiest ways to draw a path is with the shape and line tools. These tools make it easy to create symmetrical paths in common shapes. They also make a good introduction to paths and path manipulation.

Using the Rectangle Tool

In this exercise, you will draw a rectangle and a square by using the Rectangle tool, and you will select anchor points. You will also convert anchor points to curves or corners. There are no practice files for this exercise.

> **BE SURE TO** start Expression Design before beginning this exercise.

1. On the **File** menu, click **New** and create a new image 800 pixels wide and 600 pixels high, at a resolution of 96 pixels per inch. Name the file **shapes.design**, and click **OK**.

New Document

Name shapes.design

Presets 800 x 600

Width 800 px   pixels

Height 600 px

Resolution 96   px/inch

OK   Cancel

2. Press **D** on the keyboard to set the colors to the default white fill and black stroke.

3. Expression Design has four shape tools: *Rectangle*, *Ellipse*, *Polygon*, and *Line*. The shape tools are in the Toolbox in the drawing tools section. Click and hold the button (**Rectangle**, **Ellipse**, **Polygon** or **Line** button, depending on which is currently visible) to open the tool group.

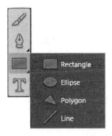

Rectangle
Ellipse
Polygon
Line

4. Click the **Rectangle** tool to select it. Click and drag anywhere on the page to make a rectangle. The size of the rectangle is defined by the dragging of the pointer on the page. Release the mouse button to complete the shape.

5. Hold [Shift] and drag out a second rectangle next to the first. Hold [Shift] to constrain the **Rectangle** tool to draw a perfect square.

You should have two shapes on the page.

Both the rectangle and the square are made up of four anchor points with straight segments connecting them.

Direct Selection

6. With the **Direct Selection** tool, click the rectangle to select it.

The path and the anchor points will be visible.

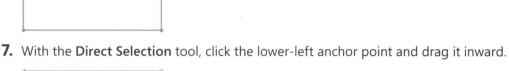

7. With the **Direct Selection** tool, click the lower-left anchor point and drag it inward.

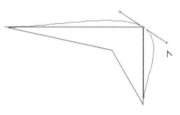

Convert
Anchor Point

8. A point can be converted to a curve or corner point by using the *Convert Anchor Point tool*. The point you moved is a corner point. In the Toolbox, click and hold to open the **Pen** tool group, and then click the **Convert Anchor Point** tool to select it.

9. With the **Convert Anchor Point** tool, click the upper-right corner point and drag out a handle to convert it from a corner point to a curve point.

10. Release the mouse button so that the control handles are displayed.

11. With the **Selection** tool, select the square you created in step 5.

You could edit it the same way you edited the rectangle, by using the Direct Selection tool, but this time, you will round the corners by using the settings in the Properties panel.

12. Look at the **Properties** panel. If the **Edit Rectangle** category is not displayed, use the scroll bars on the side of the panel to bring it into view. Expand the **Edit Rectangle** category to expose the **Corner Radius** setting.

> **Tip** Here, the square is referred to as a rectangle; Expression Design does not differentiate between squares and rectangles in this way. In fact, as you might remember from geometry class, all squares *are* rectangles.

13. With the square selected, drag the mouse pointer across the **Corner Radius** box to adjust the corner radius up to 25 pixels.

As you drag, the corners of the square will become rounded. The higher the value gets, the more rounded the corner will become.

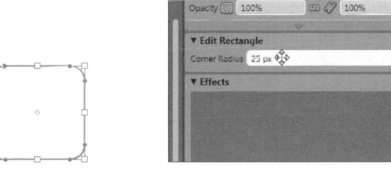

Using the Ellipse Tool

The other shape tools work the same way the Rectangle tool works. Next we'll look at the Ellipse tool.

The Ellipse tool draws an ellipse if you click and drag, or a perfect circle if you hold the Shift key while dragging. If you hold the Alt key while dragging, you will draw from the center.

In this exercise, you will use the Ellipse tool to draw a circle and an oval.

> **USE** the *shapes.design* file you created in the previous exercise.
> **OPEN** the *shapes.design* file, if it is not already open.

Ellipse

1. In the Toolbox, in the **Rectangle** tool group, choose the **Ellipse** tool.

2. Drag out an oval and a circle on a blank area on the page. The circle and oval are each composed of four anchor points connected by four curved segments.

Using the Polygon Tool

With the Polygon tool, you can make multiple-sided objects.

In this exercise, you will use the Polygon tool to draw objects with multiple sides, including stars.

> **USE** the *shapes.design* file you worked with in the previous exercise.
>
> **OPEN** the *shapes.design* file, if it is not already open.

Polygon

1. In the Toolbox, in the **Rectangle** tool group, choose the **Polygon** tool.

2. With the **Polygon** tool, click and drag anywhere in the image window to drag out a triangle. If you hold the ⌥ key as you drag, the shape will be drawn from the center.

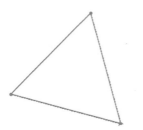

3. In the **Properties** panel, expand the **Edit Polygon** properties to alter the number of sides on the polygon. Drag the pointer across the **Points** box to change the number of sides to 5.

The polygon becomes a pentagon.

4. Change the inner depth to 50 percent.

▼ **Edit Polygon**

Points	5
Inner Depth	50%
Twirl Angle	0%

The polygon becomes a star.

Using the Line Tool

The Line tool draws straight lines. Lines can be varying widths, and they can be dashed or solid. With Expression Design, you can change the appearance of the ends of the line, and you can apply brush strokes just as you can with shapes. Brush strokes will be discussed in Chapter 7, "Using Strokes."

In this exercise, you will create lines by using the Line tool.

> **USE** the *shapes.design* file you worked with in the previous exercise.
> **OPEN** the *shapes.design* file, if it is not already open.

Line

1. In the Toolbox, in the **Rectangle** tool group, choose the **Line** tool. Click and drag to draw a straight line anywhere on the image window.

2. In the **Properties** panel, use the **Appearance** controls to change the width, and set the opacity of the line.

More

3. Click the **Show Advanced Properties** button to open the advanced options. You might have to scroll the panel to display the options.

4. Drag across the **Width** box to increase the width to **20** pixels.

   There are two other advanced options you should be aware of:

   - The Joint option sets the way the corner lines meet. This has no effect on a straight line.
   - The Caps option sets the way the line ends are rendered.

5. Choose **Round Cap** for this exercise. Notice how the ends of the line are now rounded rather than squared off.

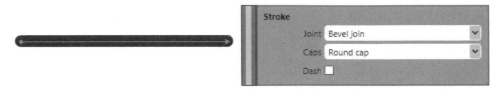

6. To make the line a dashed line, select the **Dash** check box and enter a value. The larger the value is, the farther apart (and thus longer) the dashes will be.

> **Tip** You can add a dash to any stroke on any shape.

> **CLOSE** the *shapes.design* file without saving any changes.

Using the Polyline Tool

The *Polyline tool* lets you draw Bézier paths made of segments that are either straight or curved lines. With this tool, you can draw complex sequences of curved and straight segments that would be difficult to draw with the other tools.

To draw with the Polyline tool, you start by clicking anywhere to create the first anchor point and begin the path. Then you move the pointer and click again to add a straight line segment. If you hold the Shift key as you drag, the position of the new anchor point is constrained to a 90-degree or 45-degree angle from the previous anchor point.

To create a curved segment, you move the pointer and click and drag. Holding the Shift key constrains the arc to 90, 180, or 270 degrees.

You can repeat as many times as needed to complete the path, and you can press Delete to remove anchor points if you want to back up and redo the segment. At any time, double-clicking, pressing Esc, or pressing Enter ends the path. Clicking the first anchor point creates a closed path.

In this exercise, use the Polyline tool to draw a variety of open and closed paths, following a template and using the clicking and dragging techniques, combined with modifier keys.

> **USE** the *polyline1.design* and *polyline2.design* files. These practice files are located in the *Documents\Microsoft Press\Expression Design SBS\UsingDrawingTools* folder.
>
> **BE SURE TO** click Reset Active Workspace on the Window menu before beginning this exercise.
>
> **OPEN** the *polyline1.design* file.

Path A

Polyline

1. In the Toolbox, choose the **Polyline** tool.

2. In the **Layers** panel, click **Layer 2** to make it the active layer.

3. In the **Properties** panel, change the stroke width to **3**. This will make the strokes more visible when you trace the paths.

> **Tip** If the strokes aren't bold enough for you, try increasing the stroke width to 6, 9, or even 12.

4. To make a path of straight segments, click at the starting point, then move the mouse and click to lay down additional anchor points. Follow the cues on **Path A** to make a zigzag path.

Path B

5. To make a path consisting of both straight and curved segments, use a combination of clicking and dragging. Follow the cues on **Path B** to create a closed path shaped like a pie slice.

Path C

6. **Path C** is also a path consisting of both straight and curved segments, but the curve is inward toward the center of the shape. Follow the cues on **Path C** to create the closed path.

Path D

7. Follow the cues on **Path D** to make a diamond shape.

Path E

8. With the **Polyline** tool, you can draw a circle by clicking and dragging. Follow the cues on **Path E** to draw a circle.

Path F

9. Follow the cues on **Path F** to make a simple leaf shape.

10. Close the *polyline1.design* file without saving any changes. Then on the **Window** menu, click **Reset Active Workspace**.

11. Open the *polyline2.design* file.

Path A

12. The direction and distance you drag determines the depth of the arcs when drawing curved segments. Follow the cues on **Path A** to make a shallow upward arc sequence.

Path B

13. Setting the anchor points farther away results in a deeper arc. Follow the cues on **Path B** to make a deeper upward arc sequence.

Path C

14. To make a downward arc sequence, follow the cues on **Path C**.

> **CLOSE** the *polyline2.design* file without saving any changes.

The Polyline tool is a very versatile tool, but it takes practice to learn to control it. After you are comfortable with these exercises, you will have a good idea how to control the tool and use it for your own drawings.

Using the Page Grid

The *page grid* is a non-printing grid you can use for placement. Anytime you are using any of the drawing tools, you'll find that the page grid is a good layout tool. Combined with the Snap To functions, which help you to position the mouse pointer in the document window, the grid is especially helpful to determine where to lay down the anchor points and how far to drag when you want to create a curve.

In this exercise, you will set up a page with a page grid to aid in the placement of anchor points.

> **USE** the *pentool.design* file. This practice file is located in the *Documents\Microsoft Press\ Expression Design SBS\UsingDrawingTools* folder.
>
> **BE SURE TO** click Reset Active Workspace on the Window menu before beginning this exercise.
>
> **OPEN** the *pentool.design* file.

Locked

1. In the **Layers** panel, click the **Toggle Lock** button on **Layer 1** to lock the layer.

Visibility On

2. Click the **Toggle Layer Visibility** (eyeball) button to hide the layer.

Layers
▶ Layer 1

3. On the **Edit** menu, point to **Options**, and then click **Units and Grids**.

4. In the **Options** panel, on the **Units and Grids** page, match the settings shown in the following graphic, and then click **OK**.

Options	
General	**Units**
Workspace	Document units pixels
Stroke	Stroke units pixels
Display	Type units points
Units and Grids	
Files	**Grids and guides**
Clipboard (XAML)	Grid size 32 px
Print and Export	
Memory and Undo	**Rulers**
	☑ Ruler origin is always top left of artboard
	Arrangement
	Rotation steps 8
	Nudge increment 1 px
	Stack gap size 13.33 px
	OK Cancel

5. If a grid does not display on the page, point to the **View** menu, point to **Show**, and then click **Grid**. When a feature is active, there will be a check mark beside it in the list.

Using the Pen Tool

When drawing with Bézier curves, you place anchor points and draw out handles to create tangent lines that extend from the anchor points and can be dragged to change the course of the segment. These "curves" can be straight as well as curved. Using the path tools, the Pen tool in particular, takes practice. At first you may find it totally frustrating, but it gets easier after you understand how these curves work. With practice, you will learn how to predict where the curve will fall based on how you place the anchor points, and how to create different types of anchor points, such as those shown in the following illustration.

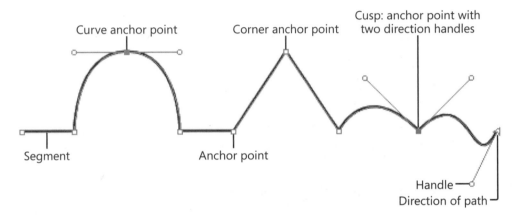

In this exercise, you will control the Pen tool by clicking and dragging to create a path. Then you will follow a template to draw a variety of open and closed paths by using the Pen tool and the modifier keys.

> **USE** the *pentool.design* file you worked with in the previous exercise.
>
> **OPEN** the *pentool.design* file, if it is not already open.

New Layer

1. In the **Layers** panel, click the **New Layer** button to create a new layer above the practice file.

Pen

2. In the Toolbox, choose the **Pen** tool.

Clicking without dragging creates a corner point. Clicking, moving the mouse, and clicking again makes a straight line.

3. Click any grid intersection. Move the mouse to the right a few squares, and click again. To constrain the line to a 90-degree angle, hold the ⌈ Shift ⌋ key when you click the second time.

4. Press ⌜Enter⌝ to end the line.

5. Clicking and dragging creates a curve. Click anywhere on the page and drag. A handle will be displayed, but no path until you click or click and drag a second time. As you draw, click and drag the handle in the direction you want the curve to go.

Direct Selection

6. Shorter control handles create shallower curves. Use the **Direct Selection** tool to drag a handle and watch the effect on the curve.

7. Clicking without dragging creates a corner point. Continue to set anchor points and draw out the handles to complete the path: as few as two, or as many as needed. Press ⌜Enter⌝ to complete the path.

Handles and anchor points can be manipulated later to place them exactly where they are needed.

8. On the **Select** menu, click **All**. Then press ⌜Del⌝ to get rid of the practice lines and curves on the page.

Visibility On

9. In the **Layers** panel, on **Template**, click the **Toggle Layer Visibility** button to make **Template** visible. Click **Layer 2** to make sure it is the active layer.

The practice exercises A through F are displayed on the page.

10. In the **Properties** panel, change the stroke width to **3**. This will make the stroke show up better when you trace the paths.

Path A

Zoom

11. In the Toolbox, choose the **Zoom** tool, and then drag a marquee around all of **Path A** to zoom in to show the points more clearly.

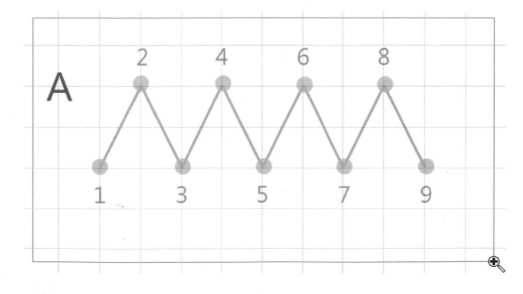

12. Follow these steps to draw your own path, tracing the path on **Template**:

    a. Click point **1** to start.

    b. Click points **2** through **9** in order.

    c. Press ⌷Enter⌷ to end the path.

Path A is an open path made entirely of straight lines. Because Template is locked, you don't have to worry about accidentally moving any of the elements of the exercise.

> **Tip** To scroll the page to display the next exercise, hold the Spacebar key to temporarily activate the Pan tool. Drag the Pan tool to reposition the document in the window.

Path B

13. Scroll the page to display **Path B**.

Path B is an open path made of curves.

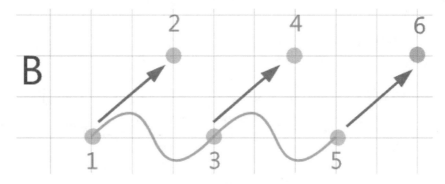

14. Follow these steps to trace the path:

    a. Click point **1** to start, and then drag to point **2** to create the control handle.

    b. Click point **3**, and then drag to point **4**.

    c. Click point **5**, drag to point **6**, and then press ⌷Enter⌷ to end the path.

> **Tip** When you drag out control handles, you can hold the Shift key to constrain them to a right angle, just as you can do when drawing a path. This can help you keep your path symmetrical.

Path C

15. Scroll the page to display **Path C**.

Path C is curved, but is made up of a combination of clicks to lay down corner points and drags to make curves. It is an open path. Notice that the drag is much shorter than it was on Path B, and therefore the handles are shorter.

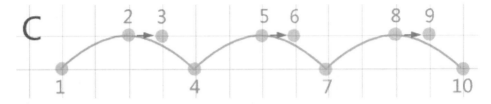

16. Follow these steps to trace the path:

    a. Click point **1** to start, click point **2**, and then drag to point **3**.

    b. Click point **4**, click point **5**, and then drag to point **6**.

    c. Click point **7**, click point **8**, and then drag to point **9**.

    d. Click point **10**, and then press Enter to end the path.

> **Tip** If you need to remove an anchor point as you are drawing, just press Delete. Pressing Delete repeatedly removes anchor points from the path in the reverse of the order they were laid down, from last to first.

Path D

17. Scroll the page to display **Path D**.

Path D is a closed path made up of corner points and curves.

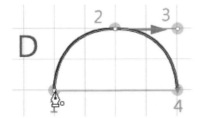

18. Follow these steps to trace the path:

    a. Click point **1** to start, click point **2**, and then drag to point **3**.

    b. Click point **4**, point to point **1**, and when the open circle is displayed beside the **Pen** pointer, click point **1** again to close the shape.

A closed path ends itself automatically when you join it to the first point.

Path E

19. Scroll the page to display **Path E**.

Path E is similar to Path C in that it consists of a combination of curves and corner points. The handles are longer, and the curves are deeper.

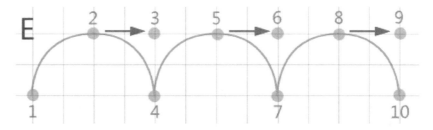

20. Follow these steps to trace the path. Try holding the [Shift] key as you drag the handles to keep them at a 90-degree angle:

   a. Click point **1** to start, click point **2**, and then drag to point **3**.

   b. Click point **4**, click point **5**, and then drag to point **6**.

   c. Click point **7**, click point **8**, and then drag to point **9**.

   d. Click point **10**, and then press [Enter] to end the path.

Path F

21. Scroll the page to display **Path F**.

Path F is a triangle, a closed path consisting of three corner points, with three straight segments.

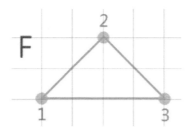

22. Follow these steps to trace the path:

   a. Click point **1** to start, click point **2**, and click point **3**.

   b. Click point **1** again to close the path.

CLOSE the *pentool.design* file without saving any changes.

Using the B-Spline Tool

The B-Spline tool lets you create Bézier paths by placing a series of anchor points in the direction you want the path to follow. Anchor points can be corner or curve points.

To use the B-Spline tool to create a path, click where you want to start the path. Use a regular click to start with a point that will create a curved segment, or hold down Alt and click to start with a corner point that will create a straight segment.

When you move the pointer, watch the thin gray line that shows where the path will fall when you click to place the anchor point. If you are holding the Shift key, the B-Spline tool will constrain the position of the next anchor point in relation to the current anchor point by 45 or 90 degrees. If you need to back up, press the Delete key.

To close a path, click the starting anchor point. To end an open path, double-click where you want the path to end, or press Esc or Enter.

In this exercise, you will follow templates to draw a variety of path shapes by using the B-Spline tool and modifier keys.

> **USE** the *B-Spline1.design* and *B-Spline2.design* files. These practice files are located in the *Documents\Microsoft Press\Expression Design SBS\UsingDrawingTools* folder.
>
> **OPEN** the *B-Spline1.design* file.

1. In the **Properties** panel, change the stroke width to 3. This will make the stroke more visible when you trace the paths.

B-Spline

2. In the Toolbox, click the **B-Spline** tool.

Path A

3. In the **Layers** panel, make sure **Layer 1** is selected.

4. Follow the cues on **Path A** to create a zigzag line. Hold down the [Alt] key and click to set the first corner anchor point. Move the pointer, and then hold down the [Alt] key and click again to create a series of straight segments with sharp corners.

Path B

5. Follow the cues on **Path B** to create a triangle. As you did in Path A, hold down the [Alt] key and click to set corner anchor points and create straight segments.

6. Click the starting anchor point to close the shape to make a triangle.

Path C

7. Follow the cues on **Path C** to create a heart. Clicking creates a curved segment. You can create a combination of curved and straight segments by using the [Alt] modifier key as before.

8. Hold down the [Alt] key and click **Point 1** to close the heart with a sharp corner point

9. Close the *B-Spline1.design* file without saving any changes, and then open the *B-Spline2.design* file.

10. In the Toolbox, click the **B-Spline** tool.

11. In the **Layers** panel, click **Layer 2**.

Path D

12. Follow the cues on **Path D** to create a half-circle.

13. Close the path by holding down the [Alt] key and clicking on the starting anchor point.

Path E

14. Follow the cues on **Path E** to create a circle.

15. Close the circle by clicking on the starting anchor point.

Path F

16. Follow the cues on **Path F** to create scallops.

17. End the scalloped path by holding down the [Alt] key and double-clicking the end point.

CLOSE the *B-Spline2.design* file without saving any changes.

Creating and Editing Cusp Points

A *cusp point* is a special anchor point that has two handles that can be manipulated independently of each other. These anchor points make inner corners possible, and let you adjust the curves for each side of a corner individually.

In this exercise, you will create and edit cusp points to create a heart from a plain circle. No practice files are required for this exercise.

> **BE SURE TO** start Expression Design before beginning this exercise.

1. On the **File** menu, click **New** to create a new document. Size isn't important.
2. If there is no grid on the page, on the **View** menu, click **Show**, and then click **Grid**.
3. On the **View** menu, click **Snap to Grid**.

Ellipse

4. In the document window, use the **Ellipse** tool to drag out a circle 12 squares wide and 12 squares tall. The top and bottom center points should be on the center vertical line of the circle.

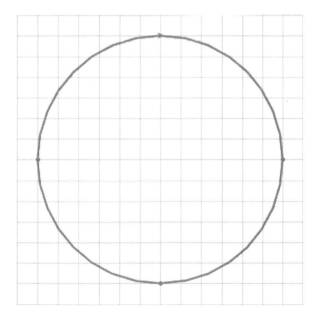

Convert
Anchor Point

5. In the **Pen** tool group in the Toolbox, choose the **Convert Anchor Point** tool. With the **Convert Anchor Point** tool, click the bottom point once to convert it to a corner point.

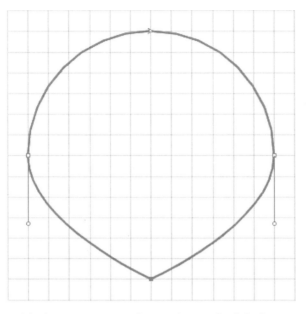

6. With the **Convert Anchor Point** tool, click the top point and drag it to the right five spaces to create a curved point with two control handles.

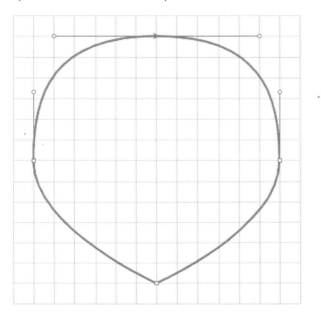

Direct Selection

7. In the Toolbox, choose the **Direct Selection** tool. Drag the top center point straight downward three squares. The shape will be flat across the top, but you will fix that in the next step.

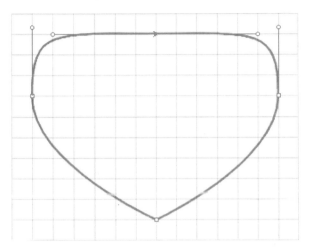

8. With the **Direct Selection** tool, hold ⌥, click the right handle of the anchor point at the top of the shape, and drag it straight upward four squares. Holding ⌥ lets the right handle move independently of the left handle. This changes the anchor point to a cusp point.

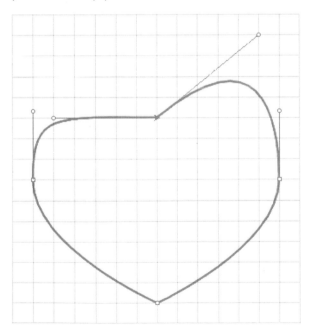

9. With the **Direct Selection** tool, drag the left handle of the anchor point at the top of the shape straight upward four squares.

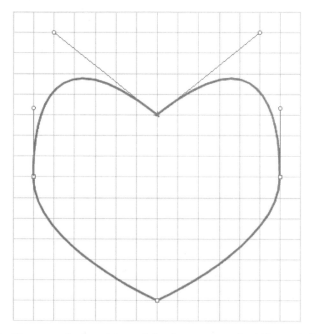

10. To smooth the sides of the heart, use the **Direct Selection** tool to click the right anchor point to expose both handles. Drag the bottom handle one square to the left (as measured by the grid). As you drag, the image window will show the outline where the new line will be.

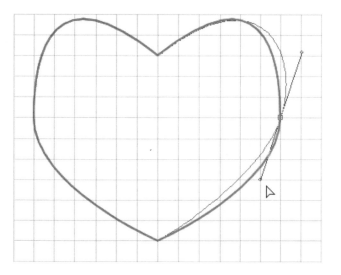

11. Click the left anchor point to expose both handles. Repeat step 10 for the left anchor point, dragging its lower handle one square to the right.

12. Save the heart as **heart.design**. You will need it in Chapter 6, "Using Fills."

> **CLOSE** the *heart.design* file.

Making Compound Paths

A compound path is made up of two or more sub-paths, each with its own starting and ending anchor points. Compound paths are most useful for making shapes with holes in them.

In this exercise, you will create compound paths by combining more than one object. You will also release a compound path to return it to two separate objects.

> **USE** the *compound_paths.design* file. This practice file is located in the *Documents\Microsoft Press\Expression Design SBS\UsingDrawingTools* folder.
>
> **OPEN** the *compound_paths.design* file.

1. In the image window, notice the two stacked circles. These circles have different fill colors.

2. Look at the **Layers** panel, on which two layers are displayed. The circles are on the **shapes** layer. Notice that there is a locked layer below, called **rectangle,** which is not visible.

3. Click the **shapes** layer in the **Layers** panel to make sure that it is active.

4. Select both circles. On the **Object** menu, click **Compound Path** and then click **Make**. The top (smaller) circle will be cut out from the bottom (larger) one.

When Expression Design creates a compound path, the hole that results is outlined with the same stroke as the object it was "punched" through.

5. Toggle the visibility of the **rectangle** layer to on to display the rectangle. Now the center of the compound path looks transparent.

6. You can convert a compound path back to its source paths. On the **Object** menu, click **Compound Path**, and then click **Release**.

After you release a path, the paths no longer have different attributes. The top path, which was punched through the bottom to make the hole, takes on the fill and stroke attributes of the bottom path.

CLOSE the *compound_paths.design* file without saving any changes.

Modifying Paths with Path Operations and Clipping

You can modify paths in a number of ways by using the path operations tools. For example, you can combine shapes to make different shapes, or you can cut out shapes from other shapes.

Using the Path Operations Commands

You can reach the Path Operations commands by clicking Path Operations on the Object menu. The following commands are available:

- *Unite* combines all selected shapes to make one shape. The new shape takes on the attributes of the front-most object. If some of the original objects are not overlapping, they keep their path shapes but act as a compound path.

- *Front Minus Back* cuts the shape of the backmost selected object out of the front-most selected object. The new shape takes on the attributes of the front-most object.

- *Back Minus Front* cuts the shape of the front-most selected object out of the backmost selected object. The new shape takes on the attributes of the bottom-most object.

- *Intersect* looks for areas where the two or more selected objects overlap. It retains the overlapping areas and deletes the rest of the shapes.

> **Tip** If the front-most object does not overlap the backmost object, or if you have three or more objects that don't all overlap in the same area, an error message will be displayed and the paths won't be affected.) The new shape takes on the attributes of the front-most object.

- *Divide* creates separate pieces based on where the shapes intersect but, unlike the Intersect command, it does not delete the shapes that do not intersect. Shapes retain their original attributes.

In this exercise, you will use various path operations on the same two shapes.

> **USE** the *path_operations.design* file. This practice file is located in the *Documents\Microsoft Press\Expression Design SBS\UsingDrawingTools* folder.
>
> **OPEN** the *path_operations.design* file.

1. In the **Layers** panel, click the **shapes** layer to make sure it is the active layer.

2. Select both the circle and the rectangle labeled **Unite**.

3. On the **Object** menu, click **Path Operations**, and then click **Unite**.

   The shapes become one and retain the attributes of the front-most shape.

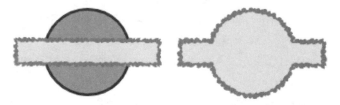

4. Select both the circle and the rectangle labeled **Front Minus Back**.

5. On the **Object** menu, click **Path Operations**, and then click **Front Minus Back**. The shape of the backmost selected object is cut out of the front-most selected object, and the overlapping areas are deleted.

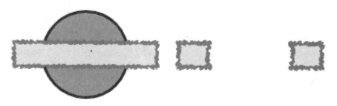

6. Select both the circle and the rectangle labeled **Back Minus Front**.

7. On the **Object** menu, click **Path Operations**, and then click **Back Minus Front**. The shape of the front-most selected object is cut out of the backmost selected object, and the overlapping areas are deleted.

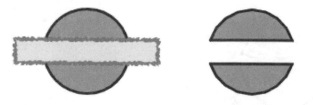

8. Select both the circle and the rectangle labeled **Intersect**.

9. On the **Object** menu, click **Path Operations**, and then click **Intersect**. The shapes are cut up based on where they overlap, and any non-overlapping areas are deleted.

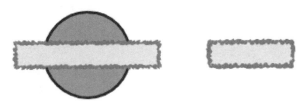

10. Select both the circle and the rectangle labeled **Divide**.

11. On the **Object** menu, click **Path Operations**, and then click **Divide**.

   The shapes are cut up based on where they overlap, but all of the pieces are retained. You can move them apart, using the Selection tool. The fill attributes are retained, and all pieces take on the stroke attributes of the front-most selected object.

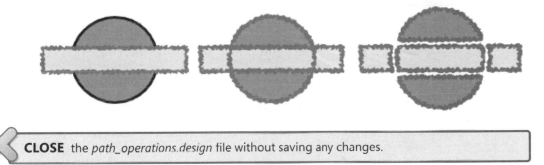

CLOSE the *path_operations.design* file without saving any changes.

Using Clipping Masks

In Expression Design, you can use one shape to mask areas in another object by grouping the objects as a *clipping mask group*. Only paths or shapes can be *clipping masks*, and you can make the mask with the top or bottom object for different results. The paths, shapes, and objects within a clipping mask group can be edited at any time, just as though they were objects within a regular group. To select just the clipping mask or one or more objects within a clipping mask group, you use the Group Select tool, the Direct Selection tool, or the Lasso Selection tool. You can then edit as desired.

You can use text as a clipping mask when you want to place an image inside the text. Because only paths and shapes can be clipping masks, the text must first be converted to outlines, ungrouped, and made into a compound path.

In this exercise, you will make a clipping mask from the top and bottom objects. Then you will convert text and use it as a clipping path.

> **USE** the *clipping_paths.design* file. This practice file is located in the *Documents\Microsoft Press\Expression Design SBS\UsingDrawingTools* folder.
>
> **OPEN** the *clipping_paths.design* file.

1. Ensure that the **shapes** layer is the selected layer.

2. Select both the rectangle and the stroke labeled **Make with Top Path**.

3. On the **Object** menu, click **Clipping Path**, and then click **Make With Top Path**.

   The top oval path masks the rectangle so that the rectangle is visible only where it is under the oval. The rest of the rectangle is now hidden, and the rectangle and oval paths are now a clipping mask group.

4. Select both the rectangle and the stroke labeled **Make with Bottom Path**.

5. On the **Object** menu, click **Clipping Path**, and then click **Make With Bottom Path**.

   The bottom rectangle path masks the oval path so that the oval path is visible only where it is on top of the rectangle. The rest of the oval path is now hidden, and the rectangle and oval paths are now a clipping mask group.

6. Clipping paths can also be released to the original objects. On the **Object** menu, click **Clipping Path**, and then click **Release**.

> **Tip** If you have used the Make With Bottom Path command, the bottom path will be on top after the clipping path is released. This is because Expression Design moves the bottom path to the top of the stack when the clipping mask is created.

7. Use the **Selection tool** to select the text **POP ART**. A bounding box will appear around the phrase.

8. On the **Object** menu, click **Convert Object To Path**. Anchor points will be displayed around the individual letters.

9. On the **Arrange** menu, click **Ungroup**. This is necessary so that the text can be made into a compound path.

10. On the **Object** menu, click **Compound Path**, and then click **Make**.

11. On the **Arrange** menu, click **Order**, and then click **Send To Back**. Only the outlines of the letters will be displayed, because they are now behind the patterned rectangle.

12. Hold the ⎡ Shift ⎤ key and click the patterned rectangle to add it to the text selection.

13. On the **Object** menu, click **Clipping Path**, and then click **Make With Bottom Path**.

CLOSE the *clipping_paths.design* file. If you are not continuing directly to the next chapter, exit Expression Design.

Key Points

- Bézier curves are composed of anchor points and line segments. Anchor points are also called nodes. Bézier curve line segments can be curved or straight.

- You can move anchor points and control handles to change the way a curve flows, and thus change the shape of the object it is part of.

- Paths can be open or closed. Open paths have two endpoints, a start point and an endpoint. On a closed path, the start point and endpoint are joined to form a closed shape.

- With the shape tools—the Rectangle tool, Ellipse tool, Polygon tool, Polyline tool, and Line tool—you can quickly draw symmetrical shapes.

- The Pen tool is one of the most versatile of the drawing tools. The Pen tool can draw curved or straight lines and combine them to create any shape.

- With the B-Spline tool, you can draw paths from control points that often lie off the contour of the shape.

- A curve point has two handles that move as one. A cusp point has two handles that can be manipulated independently of each other.

- You can set the appearance attributes of a path, including its colors, style, and thickness, in the Properties panel.

- You can use the page grid to help you align objects. Activating Snap To Grid makes alignment even easier because the anchor points you lay down snap to the grid lines.

- Use path operations to combine and separate multiple paths in different ways.

- Use clipping masks to create frame-like or window-like effects.

Chapter at a Glance

Use the Paintbrush tool, **page 126**

Use the Properties panel, **page 130**

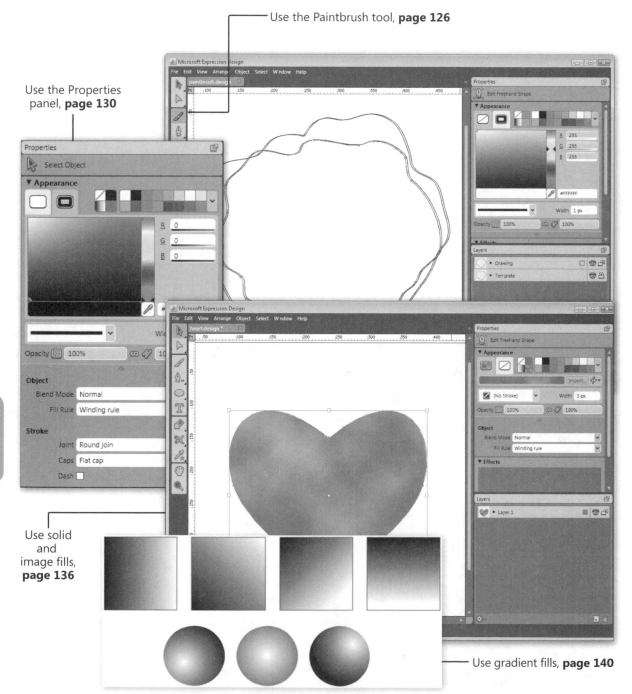

Use solid and image fills, **page 136**

Use gradient fills, **page 140**

6 Using Fills

In this chapter, you will learn to:

✔ Use the Paintbrush tool.

✔ Use the Properties panel.

✔ Use the Color Picker.

✔ Use solid and image fills.

✔ Use gradient fills.

This chapter will reveal the real potential of Microsoft Expression Design. You will learn to draw with the Paintbrush tool, which lets you draw freehand. Then you will learn to use the Properties panel to use various fill options—solid color, gradient, or image fill—to change the appearance of the objects you draw. When you change the type of fill on an object, you can change the whole mood and style of a drawing. In Expression Design you can mix colors, make custom gradients, and even import your own custom image fills.

Important Before you can use the practice files in this chapter, you need to install them from the book's companion CD to their default location. See "Using the Book's CD" at the beginning of this book for more information.

Troubleshooting Graphics and operating system–related instructions in this book reflect the Windows Vista user interface. If your computer is running Windows XP and you experience trouble following the instructions as written, please refer to the "Information for Readers Running Windows XP" section at the beginning of this book.

Using the Paintbrush Tool

Paintbrush

The Paintbrush tool lets you draw Bézier curves by clicking and dragging freehand, as if you were drawing with a pencil. To draw, just click and drag with the Paintbrush tool, and release the mouse button to end the path.

Paintbrush
Close Path

To make the path a closed path, drag the Paintbrush tool back over the starting point and release the mouse button when the white circle is displayed next to the pointer. Expression Design automatically places anchor points along the path you draw. The number of anchor points placed depends on how smoothly your shape was drawn.

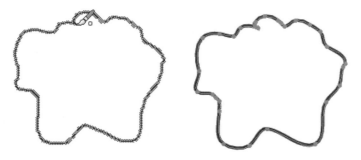

An image can have thousands of paths, and Expression Design has to remember every anchor point for every path. The more anchor points an image has, the longer the redraw time on the screen will be, and the larger the file size will be when the image is saved. When you use the Pen tool or one of the shape tools, such as the Ellipse or the Rectangle tool, Expression Design lays down the fewest number of anchor points necessary to draw the path. However, drawing with the Paintbrush tool isn't so tidy. Your hand wavers, the mouse jumps, or—if you are using a graphics tablet—the stylus might not move smoothly across the surface. Usually you will have more anchor points than necessary, and the path isn't as smooth as it could be either. *Simplifying* the path reduces the number of anchor points while retaining the shape of the path.

To simplify a path, on the Object menu, you click Simplify Path. In the dialog box, type a value or drag to set the percentage of smoothing in the Reduce By box. The default is 10 percent. When you set a higher percentage, more smoothing will take place, and the object will have fewer anchor points. Click OK to set the smoothing and evaluate the results. If you want more or less smoothing, use Ctrl+Z to undo the action, and use a different value.

The Append To Path feature lets you extend a previously drawn path. To use the Append To Path feature, you need make sure that it is turned on. On the Edit menu, click Options, and then on the Stroke panel, make sure the Drawing Tools Append To Path box is checked. The feature is on by default.

Paintbrush
Extend Path

To add to a previous path, hold the Alt key, and then point to the starting or end point of the path. When the pointer changes to the Paintbrush with a plus sign, click and drag to extend the path. If you want to close the path, continue dragging to the other end point and release the mouse button when the open circle shows by the Paintbrush pointer.

> ## Enhance Your Drawing Experience with a Graphics Tablet
>
> A graphics tablet is a great addition to any graphics program, and Expression Design is no exception. Instead of using a mouse, you draw on a tablet with a pen-like stylus. Because the stylus responds to pressure and tilt, you have the feel of drawing with pencil and paper, with better control over the design. Tablets come in various sizes and styles, with varying levels of pressure. The pricing varies according to features and size. To use pressure sensitivity with Expression Design, on the Edit menu, click Options, and on the Stroke panel, select the Enable Pressure Sensitivity box.

In this exercise, you will use the Paintbrush tool to draw a rose.

> **USE** the *paintbrush.design* file. This practice file is located in the *Documents\ Microsoft Press\Expression Design SBS\UsingFills* folder.
>
> **BE SURE TO** start Expression Design before beginning this exercise, click Reset Active Workspace on the Window menu, and press D to set Expression Design to the default color, fill, and stroke before beginning this exercise.
>
> **OPEN** the *paintbrush.design* file.

Paintbrush

1. In the Toolbox, choose the **Paintbrush** tool.

None

2. In the **Properties** panel, click the **None** button as the fill color.

3. In the **Layers** panel, make sure the **Drawing** layer is selected.

4. Click and drag to loosely trace the larger shape from the **Template** layer to the **Drawing** layer. Be sure to close the shape.

5. Click and drag to loosely trace the smaller shape from the **Template** layer to the **Drawing** layer. The circles can overlap some; a little overlap makes a better rose. Be sure to close the shape.

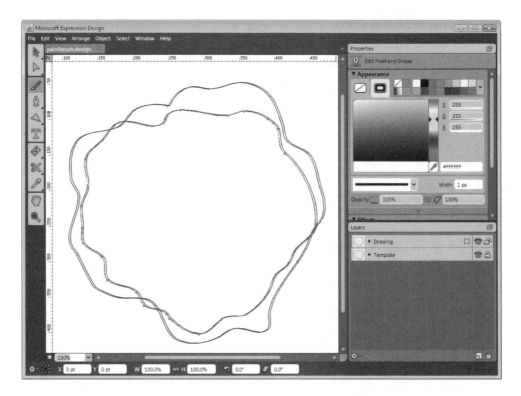

Visibility On

6. Click the **Toggle Layer Visibility** (eyeball) button to hide the contents of the layer.

Selection

7. Use the **Selection** tool to select both shapes. On the **Edit** menu, click **Copy** to copy the shapes to the Clipboard; then, on the **Edit** menu, click **Paste in Front** to paste the copies on the page.

Your image will not look any different, because the Paste in Front command places the copies directly on top of the originals. Make sure not to click on the page; you want the two new shapes to remain selected.

> **Tip** If you accidentally deselect the shapes, use the Layers panel to select them by holding the Shift key and clicking on them in the panel.

8. Hold both ⌥ (to resize from the center) and ⇧ (to constrain the proportions of the shape), and click and drag inward on a corner of the bounding box to make the shapes slightly smaller than the originals.

Rotate

9. Point outside a corner of the bounding box, and when the pointer turns into the rotate pointer, click and drag to rotate the new shapes slightly.

10. Repeat the following sequence three more times so that the original shapes are almost filled with smaller and rotated copies of the circles:

- On the **Edit** menu, click **Copy**.
- On the **Edit** menu, click **Paste in Front**
- Resize the copies slightly smaller.
- Rotate the copies slightly.

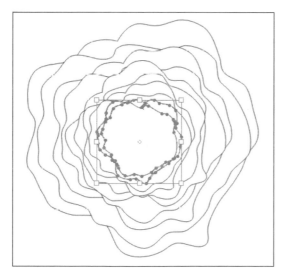

11. Draw two or three smaller shapes in the center to fill in the middle of the rose. Now that you have the basic rose shape, click **Save As** on the **File** menu, and save your file as **my_rose.design**.

You will need this file for a future exercise in this chapter.

CLOSE the *paintbrush.design* and *my_rose.design* files.

Using the Properties Panel

The Properties panel is where the magic happens. Up to now, we have used it only for the most basic changes and have barely begun to explore the options that can turn a simple drawing into something unique.

The Properties panel is dynamic. At the top of the Properties panel is the *Color Picker*, which is used to set the colors for fills and strokes and to choose image fills. The Color Picker has a *Fill tab* that lets you choose colors for object fills, and a *Stroke tab* that lets you choose stroke colors. The Color Picker is always visible. The categories it displays vary, depending on whether or not there is a selection on the document and if so, what kind of object is selected. For example, if a text object is selected, the Text category is available. If a path is selected, you will have an Effects category, but no Text category. This keeps the Properties panel from becoming crowded with extraneous settings you don't need at the time.

Tip If your Properties panel feels a bit cramped, you can press the F4 key to hide the Layers panel temporarily. Press F4 again to make the Layers panel come back.

In this exercise, you will use the different settings within the categories of the Properties panel to alter your document.

USE the *properties_panel.design* file. This practice file is located in the *Documents\ Microsoft Press\Expression Design SBS\UsingFills* folder.

BE SURE TO click Reset Active Workspace on the Window menu before beginning this exercise.

OPEN the *properties_panel.design* file.

---

1. Press D to make sure your stroke and fill attributes are set to the defaults.

When there is nothing selected on the page, only the Appearance category of the Properties panel is visible. One of the features of the Appearance category is the Color Picker.

2. From the **Window** menu, click **Layers** to close the **Layers** panel. This temporary move will leave more room for the **Properties** panel to expand.

Collapse

> **Tip** You can collapse a category to its title bar by clicking the Collapse arrow to the left of its name. This is especially helpful when you have the Layers panel visible. This arrow acts as a toggle, letting you collapse or expand categories as desired.

Show
Advanced
Properties

3. A category often includes a **Show Advanced Properties** arrow, which acts as a toggle to expand and collapse the category's advanced options. Click the **Show Advanced Properties** arrow to extend the panel and show the advanced options.

The panel now displays the extended options for the Appearance category. Depending on the size of your computer screen, you may have to scroll to display these options.

There are two options that can be set here. The first is Blend Mode, which is set to Normal. Blend Mode affects how objects react to the colors of objects below them. The second is Fill Rule, which is set by default to Winding Rule. The fill rule affects how an object is filled if it is a compound path or a single path that crosses over itself. The two choices are Winding Rule and Even-Odd Rule.

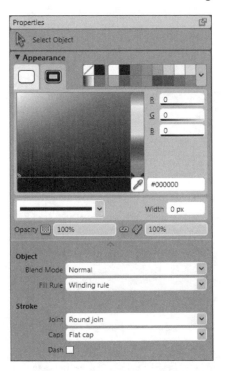

Selection

4. You can understand how these fill rules work by applying them to the squiggle shape on the practice file. The shape crosses over itself, and currently has a 2-pixel stroke and no fill. Use the **Selection** tool to select the freehand line shape.

5. In the **Color Picker**, click the **Fill** tab, then click the red color swatch to fill the shape with red.

The default fill rule, the Winding Rule, fills the whole shape with red, even though you typically would expect a hole where the path contains a loop that falls inside the path.

6. With the shape still selected, choose **Even-odd** from the **Fill Rule** list in the **Properties** panel. The fill now ignores the "hole."

7. Fill rules also affect compound shapes. Select both circles on the practice file and convert them to a compound shape by clicking **Compound Path** on the **Object** menu, and then clicking **Make**.

The result is the donut shape shown on the left in the following image. Notice also in the Properties panel that when you create a compound path, Expression Design automatically sets the fill rule to Even-Odd so that the hole is created. If you choose Winding Rule from the Fill Rule list in the Properties panel, the fill ignores the "hole" and fills the whole path, as shown on the right in the following graphic. The circles look like one object, but both paths are visible when the object is selected.

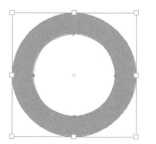 

8. Use the **Selection** tool to select the text on the practice file.

Expression Design adds a Text category with text options to the Properties panel. (Note also that advanced options are available.) If you wanted to, you could not only change the fill and stroke options of the text using the Properties panel, but the font and size of the text as well. The text options will be discussed in Chapter 8, "Working with Text."

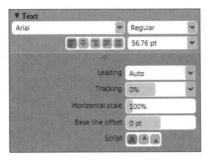

Below the Text category is the Effects category. This category is available when any object is selected. It lets you add fully editable and reversible special effects called Live Effects to your drawing. These range from common effects like bevels and drop shadows to artistic effects like Ink Outlines and Stained Glass.

CLOSE the *properties_panel.design* file without saving any changes.

Using the Color Picker

You've had a look at the Appearance category, and used the Color Picker for basic fill color changes. You can use these settings to change the fills to solid colors, gradient fills, or image fills, and also to change the opacity of strokes and fills. There are three kinds of fills: solid, gradient, and image fills.

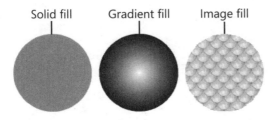

Solid fill   Gradient fill   Image fill

You click the Fill tab to set or change the fill color, and click the Stroke tab to set or change the stroke color.

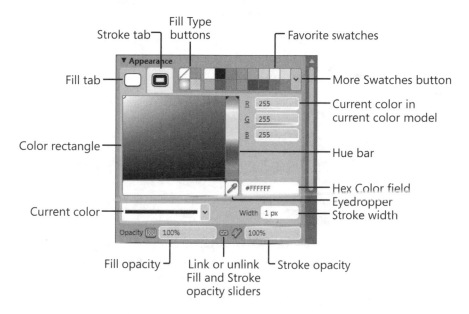

Click any of the following four fill type buttons to set the kind of fill or stroke:

Fill button	Function
None	Click the None button to remove the color from a fill or stroke. The object is transparent when the color is removed.
Solid Color	Click the Solid Color button for a solid color fill or stroke.
Gradient Color	Click the Gradient Color button for a gradient fill or stroke.
Image Fill	Click the Image Fill button to use one of the repeating bitmap images as a fill. These can be from the swatches that come with Expression Design, or you can import your own images to use as fills.

To choose colors for solid fills, you can use any one of the following methods:

- Click one of the swatches in the favorite color palette. You can open the Swatches Gallery by clicking the More Swatches button for more choices.

- Click in the color rectangle to choose a color. To choose a color from the color rectangle, slide or click on the Hue bar slider to the right of the color rectangle, then click inside the color rectangle to set a custom color. A white circle indicates the location in the rectangle of the current color.

- Click the eyedropper, then click anywhere on the program window to sample a color. You can even click on the Expression Design interface!

- Click the Hex Color field and type in a hexadecimal value, also called a hex code, or drag in the color rectangle to choose a hexadecimal color. Hexadecimal colors are used for Web design. You can highlight the value and copy and paste it into your Web design program.

Expression Design lets you select a fill or stroke color based on five color models: *HLS*, *HSB*, *RGB*, *CMYK*, and *Hex*. CMYK is used most often for professional offset printing. If you plan to print your work at home or post the illustrations on the Web, you should use RGB, which is the default setting. To choose a color model, click any of the labels for the current color model (for example, click R, G, or B) and choose the color model you prefer. The hexadecimal code is always available in the Hex Color field no matter what color model is chosen.

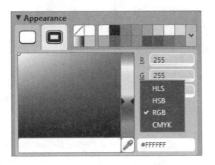

Using Solid and Image Fills

The fill of an object can completely change the style of the illustration, and Expression Design gives you a lot of choices. One more choice is to import custom image fills of your own, giving you a one-of-a-kind pattern fill.

In this exercise, you will add solid and image fills to objects using the heart you drew in Chapter 5, "Using the Drawing Tools."

USE the *heart.design* file you created and saved in Chapter 5. If you did not create the file, use the *heart.design* practice file. This file is located in the *Documents\Microsoft Press\ Expression Design SBS\UsingFills* folder.

BE SURE TO click Reset Active Workspace on the Window menu before beginning this exercise.

OPEN the *heart.design* file.

Selection

1. Use the **Selection** tool to select the heart.

> **Tip** Stroke and fill colors will be applied to the selected object only. If multiple objects are selected, Expression Design applies the color to all of the selected objects when you choose a stroke or fill color in the Color Picker.

None

2. Click the **Fill** tab, and then click the red color swatch. Click the **Stroke** tab and click the **None** fill type button to remove the color from the stroke.

3. To set a custom fill color not in the favorite swatches palette, click the **Fill** tab, then drag the pointer in the color rectangle. The fill color of the heart changes as you drag.

4. Drag the slider on the **Hue** bar, and notice that the color changes on the fill of the heart as you drag.

These dynamic changes are very helpful when you are trying to choose the right color or shade of a color, because the color of the object is displayed in relation to the rest of the illustration.

5. Look at the current color area under the color rectangle. It is now split, showing the initial color and the current color. If you don't like the color change, you can click the initial color to revert to it.

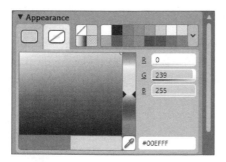

Image Fill

6. Click the **Image Fill** button to use the last-used image fill.

7. Choose a fill from the **Swatches Gallery**. To do so, click the **More Swatches** arrow next to the favorite swatches palette to open the **Swatches Gallery** and scroll through the choices.

You'll find solid colors, gradients, and image fills, including stone, metal, or wood fills.

8. Make sure the **Fill** tab is active, and then click any of the image fills in the **Swatches Gallery** to fill the heart with an image fill.

Notice that as you try various fills, they are added to the Most Recent palette in the Swatches Gallery. You can revert to any of these fills by clicking the swatch.

Not only can you use the image fills that are shipped with Expression Design, you can import your own custom image fills. When the fill type is set to Image Fill, the Appearance category includes an Import button. Clicking the Import Button lets you import your own images to use as image fills.

Import...

9. Click the **Import** button and navigate to the folder to which your CD practice files have been installed.

10. Click the *pattern.bmp* file, and then click **Open**.

The heart will be filled with the new pattern, and the Image Fill button will exhibit the new pattern as well. You can also add image fills by clicking the options list at the bottom of the Swatches Gallery and choosing Add Image Swatch.

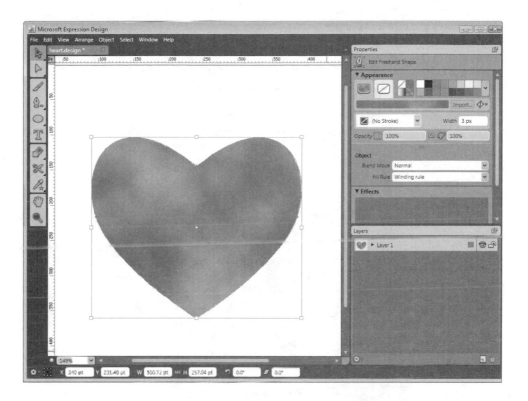

> **Tip** When you import an image fill from another location, Expression Design links to that file. It doesn't embed the image into the document, so if you move or delete the original file or open the document on another computer, the image fill will not show.

If the image you have selected as an image fill is smaller than the object you are filling, the fill will be repeated to fill up the space, so a self-contained image that looks good when it repeats or tiles in this fashion works best as an image fill. You can edit the fill to fit the object by using the Fill Transform tool.

Fill Transform

11. Click and drag on the object with the **Fill Transform** tool to reposition the fill in the object. This action repositions only the fill; it does not affect the position of the object.

Rotate

12. Point the **Fill Transform** tool outside any bounding box corner until the pointer turns into the rotate pointer, then click and drag to rotate. This action rotates only the fill, not the object.

Scale

13. Point the **Fill Transform** tool on any bounding box corner until the pointer turns into the double-headed scale pointer, then drag inward to size the pattern smaller or outward to size the pattern larger on the object. This does not affect the size or shape of the object itself, only the fill.

> **Tip** When you transform an object by scaling, rotating, or skewing, the image fill is also transformed. This feature is on by default, but you can turn it off on the Edit menu by clicking Options. On the General page, deselect the Transform Image Fill check box.

If you prefer to type transformation values manually, you can use the Transform menu to the right of the Import button.

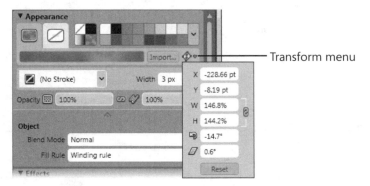

Transform menu

14. Use the **Save As** command to save the *heart.design* file as **my_heart.design**. You will need it in an exercise later in this chapter.

CLOSE the *heart.design* and *my_heart.design* files.

Using Gradient Fills

The last kind of fill is the gradient fill. Gradients are a blend of several colors, gradually blending together. Gradients can give the illusion of depth to two-dimensional objects, and can lend an air of realism to your illustrations. Gradients can be applied to any fill or basic stroke. You can customize them by changing their color, angle, or transparency, or choosing between different kinds of gradients.

Gradient Color

To apply a gradient to an object, select one or more objects. Then, in the Color Picker, click the Fill or Stroke tab, and click the Gradient Color fill type button. Expression Design applies the default black-to-white linear gradient to the object or objects.

To choose a preset gradient, click the More Swatches button on the Color Picker and choose a gradient from the swatches.

After you apply a gradient, the gradient bar appears under the color rectangle. There are two gradient shapes, linear and radial. You can click the radial button to change the gradient shape.

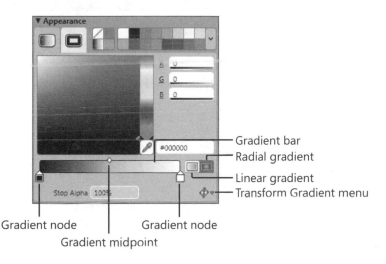

Gradient bar
Radial gradient
Linear gradient
Transform Gradient menu

Gradient node   Gradient node
          Gradient midpoint

Gradient Node

Each color contained in the gradient has a *gradient node* (also known as a *color stop*). Moving the gradient nodes affects the *speed* of the gradient—that is, how quickly it blends into the next color in the gradient bar. You click and drag the gradient nodes to adjust the blending of the gradient. The gradient nodes are also used to change the colors of the gradient. To do this, you select a node, and then choose a color from the color rectangle. To use a swatch as the new color, select the gradient node, then hold the Alt key while clicking on the swatch.

Midpoint Slider

You drag the *midpoint slider* to specify the halfway point between colors or transparency. This affects how the colors of the gradient blend.

Gradients can have transparency. This is set using the ***Stop Alpha slider***. You select a gradient node, and then drag the Stop Alpha slider to set the degree of transparency. Transparency can be set for each gradient node individually. Select the gradient node on which you want to adjust the transparency, and adjust the Stop Alpha slider.

The Gradient Transform tool in the Toolbox lets you specify how a gradient is positioned on an object. To transform a linear gradient, select an object with a linear gradient fill or stroke, then click and drag with the Gradient Transform tool in the direction you want the gradient to flow.

Gradient
Transform

> **Tip** You can find the Gradient Transform tool in the same group as the Fill Transform tool.

The same principle applies to a radial gradient. You can use the Gradient Transform tool to move the highlight of a radial gradient to give the illusion of a three-dimensional figure in some cases. This is particularly effective when you are using a gradient with a lot of contrast between colors, like the white-to-black gradient used in this illustration:

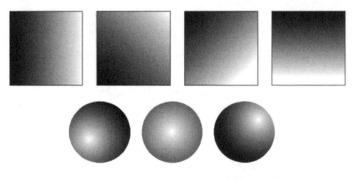

In this exercise, you will use gradient fills to give a realistic fill to the rose you created earlier in this chapter.

> **USE** the *my_rose.design* file you created and saved earlier in this chapter. If you did not create this file, you can use the *my_rose.design* practice file. This file is located in the *Documents\Microsoft Press\Expression Design SBS\UsingFills* folder.
>
> **BE SURE TO** click Reset Active Workspace on the Window menu and then press D to set the colors to the defaults before beginning this exercise.
>
> **OPEN** the *my_rose.design* file.

Gradient Color

1. On the **Select** menu, click **All** to select all of the rose shapes.

2. On the **Color Picker**, click the **Fill** tab, and then click the **Gradient Color** button. All of the shapes are filled with the current gradient.

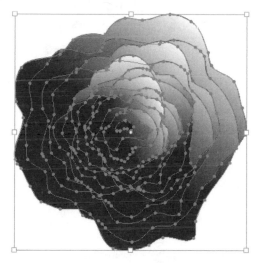

3. On the **Gradient** bar, click the leftmost gradient node to select it. Move the **Hue** bar slider to change the color rectangle to red if necessary, and then drag the pointer in the color rectangle to choose a dark red. Make a note of this color's hexadecimal description; ours is **#9B0404**. You'll need this information in a later step.

Gradient Node

4. On the **Gradient** bar, click the rightmost gradient node to select it.

5. Next to the **Hue** bar, click in the **Hex Color** field, and type the hexadecimal value of the previous color. Press the Enter key to change the color of the current gradient node to that of the opposite gradient node.

Selection

6. Click again to return to the **Selection** tool. The rose shapes turn completely red because you now have a red-to-red gradient.

7. Add another gradient node to the **Gradient** bar by clicking on the bottom edge of bar, at the center.

Notice that you now have two midpoint sliders rather than one. No matter how many gradient nodes are on the Gradient bar, there will be a midpoint slider between each of them so they can always be adjusted individually.

You can remove gradient nodes you no longer want or need by clicking them and dragging them away from the Gradient bar.

8. The new gradient node is also red. To change the color, select the node, hold the Alt key, and click once on the black swatch in the favorites at the top of the **Color Picker**. There is now a red-to-black-to-red gradient both on the **Gradient** bar and on your rose shapes.

Radial

9. Use Ctrl+H to hide the edges and anchor points of the shapes so that the effect of the gradient on the rose is easier to see. Change the gradient shape from linear to radial by clicking the **Radial** button. This makes a big difference in the gradient placement on the rose.

10. In the Toolbox, choose the **Selection** tool.

Even though the edges and anchor points on the rose shapes aren't displayed because we hid them in the previous step, the pieces are still selected. Ctrl+H acts as a toggle to hide and show edges. You achieve the same effect by looking under Show in the View menu and clicking Hide.

11. Use Ctrl + H to show the edges, and then deselect all pieces by opening the **Select** menu and clicking **Deselect**.

12. Click on the largest of the rose shapes to select it.

Gradient
Transform

13. In the Toolbox, select the **Gradient Transform** tool and click in the approximate center of the rose, then drag outward to the edge of the rose shape.

Because only the outer rose shape is selected, the tool will affect only it and disregard the other rose shapes. If you don't like the way the gradient falls on the shape, you can redo it; each drag will replace the last, so you can try as many times as necessary to get a look you are happy with. Try dragging to the edge of the shape, and try stopping before you get to the edge. You will get very different results.

14. Repeat this process, selecting one rose shape at a time and using the **Gradient Transform** tool to reposition the gradient on each shape.

> **Tip** Hold down Ctrl to switch to the Selection tool temporarily. Release this key to return to whatever tool you most recently clicked in the Toolbox.

15. On the **Select** menu, click **All** so the whole rose is selected. Then in the **Color Picker**, click the **Stroke** tab. Click the **None** button to remove the stroke from all of the rose shapes.

Nonel

16. If you wish, duplicate the rose and try different color combinations for the gradient. You could try peach and light yellow to make the rose look like a Peace rose, or try pink and white. Then save your rose as **my_gradient_rose.design**.

CLOSE all open documents. If you are not continuing directly on to the next chapter, quit Expression Design.

Key Points

● The Paintbrush tool lets you draw freehand, as if you are using a pencil.

● You can fill the objects you draw with a variety of fills: solid colors, gradients, and even image fills.

● You can use the Gradient bar to mix custom gradients.

● You can import custom image fills to use your own images.

Chapter at a Glance

Set stroke attributes and use the Strokes Gallery, **page 150**

Edit paths
to change
stroke appearance,
page 153

Create and save custom
strokes, **page 158**

Use the Blend Paths
command, **page 165**

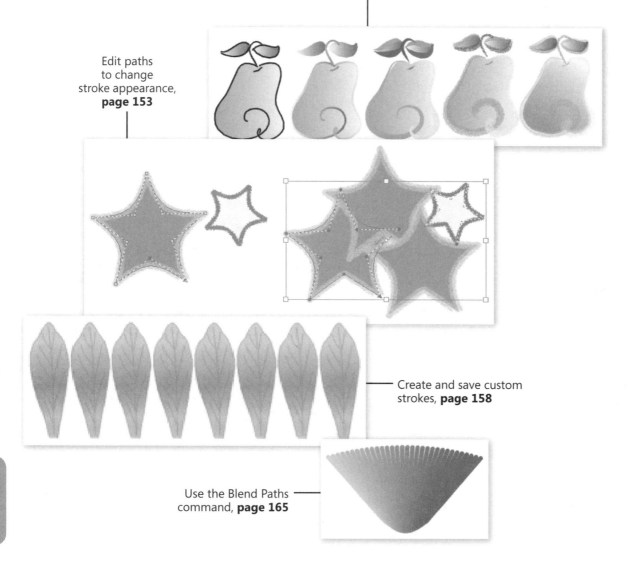

7 Using Strokes

In this chapter, you will learn to:

✔ Set stroke attributes and use the Strokes Gallery.

✔ Edit paths to change stroke appearance.

✔ Create and save custom strokes.

✔ Use the Blend Paths command.

This chapter will show you the strength of the Microsoft Expression Design strokes feature. By changing the type of *brush stroke* and its width, you can make the same illustration look like a watercolor painting or a cartoon drawing; the possibilities are endless!

In this chapter, you will learn to create vector and image custom strokes, and how to anchor and repeat strokes. You will also learn how to *blend paths*, taking two or more objects and blending them together to create a series of steps in between. You will also learn to use clipping paths to make two objects look interlinked.

Important Before you can use the practice files in this chapter, you need to install them from the book's companion CD to their default location. See "Using the Book's CD" at the beginning of this book for more information.

Troubleshooting Graphics and operating system–related instructions in this book reflect the Windows Vista user interface. If your computer is running Windows XP and you experience trouble following the instructions as written, please refer to the "Information for Readers Running Windows XP" section at the beginning of this book.

Setting Stroke Attributes and Using the Strokes Gallery

Much of Expression Design's versatility is due to *skeletal strokes*, also referred to as *brush strokes*, a concept created by Creature House co-founder Alex Hsu. Skeletal strokes were the basis for the first version of Creature House Expression, a program that evolved into the advanced illustration program you are working with now, Expression Design. These strokes are placed along a vector path, following curves and twists. They can be edited as a whole or one anchor point at a time, and they can mimic a variety of natural media or be composed of images.

Expression Design has two types of strokes: the basic stroke and the brush strokes. The basic stroke follows the path with a uniform thickness. You can change its width and color, and it can be either a solid color or a gradient. All other strokes are brush strokes, which can be anything from strokes that have soft edges to strokes that mimic artistic media such as a calligraphic pen or watercolors. You can also use brush strokes that are defined from bitmap images; these are called image strokes. Strokes are stored in the Strokes Gallery, which is found on the Properties panel, in the Appearance category below the Color Picker. To the right of the Strokes Gallery is the Stroke Width box. When you combine strokes from the gallery with width, opacity, and dash settings, the possibilities are almost limitless.

In this exercise, you will set stroke attributes by using the Color Picker and by choosing a brush stroke from the Strokes Gallery.

> **USE** the *my_heart.design* file you created and saved in Chapter 6. If you did not create the file, use the *my_heart.design* practice file. This file is located in the *Documents\Microsoft Press\Expression Design SBS\UsingStrokes* folder.
>
> **BE SURE TO** start Expression Design before beginning this exercise.
>
> **OPEN** the *my_heart.design* file.

1. In the **Properties** panel, in the **Appearance** category, click the **Stroke** tab to set stroke attributes.

   > **Tip** To set a solid stroke color, use the same methods you used to set a solid fill color. (See Chapter 6, "Using Fills," for a refresher.) You can also choose a gradient swatch for a gradient stroke.

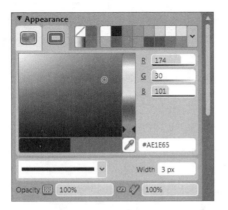

2. Click the arrow to open the **Strokes Gallery**.

The basic stroke, which is the default, is at the top of the list in the favorites section. The other strokes are grouped according to type.

3. With the heart selected, click a stroke in the **Strokes Gallery** to apply it. Adjust the width of the stroke by using the **Stroke Width** box. For now, choose the basic stroke and set the width to **10** pixels.

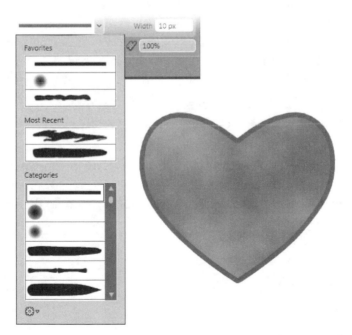

In the Properties panel, in the advanced properties, there are additional stroke options. You can choose how strokes are joined at corners, and you can select the endcap style. Strokes can also be dashed lines. To display these options, click the Show Advanced Properties button at the bottom of the Appearance category. You may have to scroll down to see the additional options.

4. Ensure that the heart is selected. In the **Properties** panel, in the advanced properties, select the **Dash** check box. Enter **10** in the **Space** box. This determines how far
apart the dashes are.

You should now have a heart with a dashed outline.

5. Try the other **Joint** and **Caps** options. The heart in the following graphic was created
with the **Round Join** and **Round Cap** options, and with a spacing of 10 pixels.

You can set the opacity of strokes and fills in the Appearance category just below
the Strokes Gallery. The 100 percent setting makes the stroke or fill completely
opaque. The 0 percent setting makes the stroke or fill completely transparent. To
change the value for the fill and stroke equally, click the link button between the
two values; to set separate values for fill and stroke opacity, unlink them.

6. Experiment with the different strokes in the **Strokes Gallery**. Try at least one stroke
from each category. Experiment with colors and widths, with and without the **Dash**
feature.

A single illustration can have many different styles, depending on the styles of the
strokes and fills you use. The simple pear clip art in the following image has had
various strokes added to it. As this example shows, changing the stroke can change
the whole style of the drawing.

CLOSE the *my_heart.design* file without saving any changes.

Editing Paths to Change Stroke Appearance

There are other commands that can change the stroke appearance. ***Reversing a path*** reverses the start point and endpoint so that the path runs in the opposite direction. This is helpful when you want a tapered brush stroke to face the opposite direction. The Reverse Path tool is found in the Toolbox under the ***Scissors tool***. Click and hold the Scissors tool to reveal the tool group. Reverse a path by clicking anywhere on a selected path with the Reverse Path tool.

Reverse Path

Clicking the Reverse Path command on the Object menu will also reverse any selected path. The end of a path is always shown as an arrow, which indicates the direction the path is flowing. Notice the arrow position on the two paths in the following image.

Scissors

You can make multiple paths from one original path by ***Splitting the path***. With the Scissors tool, you can cut one path into multiple segments. You do not have to cut on an anchor point to split a path; the path can be split anywhere, but the path has to be selected in order to be split. In the image that follows, the original path is on the left. The center path shows the path split once, and the path on the right was split multiple times.

Start Point

The ***Start point*** of a path can be changed to any anchor point on the path. With an open path, it is easy to find where the start point of a path is, but closed paths have start points too. These are used to determine how brush strokes flow along the shape. Use the Start Point tool (also located under the Scissors tool) to click any point of a selected closed path to change the start point and the flow of the stroke.

The start point for an open path can be changed by selecting the path and clicking any point with the Start Point tool. (If you click the existing start point of a closed path with the Start Point tool, the start point doesn't change, but the path is reversed, the same as using the Reverse Path tool.) If you click any other point on the path with the Start Point tool, the path will change to a closed path. In the image that follows, the path on the left is the original arc. The center arc had its starting point changed to the anchor point on the right side of the arc; and the one on the right had the starting point changed to the bottom anchor point.

Converting a stroke to a path changes the stroke into an independent object. You can then apply strokes to it. In the following image, the stroke on the left has a tapered ink stroke applied to it. On the right, the stroke was converted to a path by clicking Convert Stroke To Path from the Object menu. The Big Wave stroke was then added from the Design Elements 1 collection found in the Strokes Gallery.

Clones and duplicates sound as if they are the same thing, and in some ways they are. They are both copies of an object. Both duplicates and clones can have their strokes and fills altered without affecting the original; and both can be moved on the page or scaled or transformed without affecting the original. The difference is that a duplicate has no ties to the object it was copied from, but a *clone* does. A clone is a special kind of object that is based on its original master path. Clones do not have anchor points, and their shapes cannot be edited. Once an object is cloned, the original object becomes the master, and any editing to the anchor points on the master also changes the clone.

In the following image, the master is the one on the left. On the right is the clone. They have different fills and strokes, and the clone has been scaled down and rotated. The master has five corner points, and so does the clone. When two anchor points on the master were converted to curve points, the corresponding points on the clone were converted to curve points at the same time. Because of the rotation of the clone, they may not seem to be the same points that were converted on the master, but Expression Design remembers which points correspond no matter how many transformations you make to the clone. This is a much easier concept to grasp when doing it yourself rather than reading about how it works!

In this exercise, you will reverse and split paths and change their start points. You will also convert a stroke to a path, and you will work with both a duplicate and a clone.

> **USE** the *paths_and_clones.design* file. This practice file is located in the *Documents\ Microsoft Press\Expression Design SBS\UsingStrokes* folder.
>
> **OPEN** the *paths_and_clones.design* file.

Selection

1. Use the **Selection** tool to select the path labeled **Reversing the Stroke**. When you first select the path, a bounding box is displayed around the stroke.

Reverse Path

2. In the Toolbox, click the **Reverse Path** tool. As soon as you click the **Reverse Path** tool, the bounding box disappears and the path of the stroke is visible. Click anywhere on the stroke to reverse it.

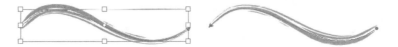

3. Keeping the path selected, on the **Object** menu, click **Reverse Path**. The path reverses again. The menu command works exactly the same as the **Reverse Path** tool in the Toolbox, and the stroke will look as it did originally.

4. Use the **Selection Tool** to select the path labeled **Splitting the Path**. As before, when you first select the path, the bounding box will be displayed around the stroke.

Scissors

5. In the Toolbox, click the **Scissors** tool. As soon as you click the **Scissors** tool, the bounding box disappears and the path of the stroke is visible. Click the center anchor point to split the path into two paths.

After you use the Scissors tool, the path segments are individual objects and each can be selected and manipulated independently of the other.

The Scissors tool can be used only on a path that is selected. You must click the path, but you do not have to click an anchor point. Each time you click, the path segment will divide into two segments. You can divide a path as many times as you want.

6. With the **Start Point** tool, you can change the start point of an open or closed path. The stroke must be selected in order to change its start point. With the **Selection** tool, select the closed circular stroke labeled **Changing the Starting Point**. The stroke will be surrounded with a bounding box. As you know, the direction of a stroke is indicated by an arrow on the endpoint, so you can tell that this stroke goes in a clockwise direction.

Start Point

7. In the Toolbox, click the **Start Point** tool. The bounding box is removed to display the path more clearly. Click the start point of the stroke. It will change direction to move counterclockwise.

8. Any anchor point on a path can become the start point. Click the right anchor point with the **Start Point** tool so that the starting point moves to the side of the circle.

9. With the **Selection** tool, select the open path labeled **Changing the Starting Point**.

10. Use the **Start Point** tool to click the start point or endpoint of the open path. The direction of the path is reversed. On an open path, changing the start point is the same as reversing the path.

11. Strokes can be converted to paths. After conversion, the stroke is an object and can have fills and strokes the same as any other object. With the **Selection** tool, click the stroke labeled **Convert a Stroke to a Path**. The bounding box is displayed around the stroke.

12. On the **Object** menu, click **Convert Stroke To Path**. Expression Design places anchor points around the stroke.

13. Edit the stroke the same as you would any object, changing fills and adding a stroke.

14. When you use clones, you can edit the shapes of multiple copies of an object at once. Although they can have different fills and strokes and can be scaled and transformed independently, clones do not have anchor points and therefore cannot be edited. Use the **Selection** tool to select the star labeled **Using Clones**.

15. On the **Edit** menu, click **Clone** to clone the star. The clone is placed up and slightly to the right of the master and is selected, with a bounding box around it.

> **Tip** Notice that a clone does not have anchor points.

16. Drag the clone away from the master so it is out of the way. Change the stroke and fill, and rotate or scale the clone if you want. Notice that the master doesn't change in any way when you make changes to the clone.

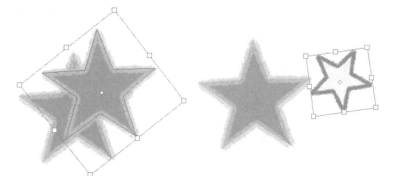

Direct Selection

Convert
Anchor Point

17. Select the master, and then use the **Direct Selection** tool or the **Convert Anchor Point** tool to alter the anchor points on two of the points of the star. I used the **Convert Anchor Point** tool to convert the master path's inner corners to curves.

As each change is made to the master, the corresponding points on the clone change, too.

18. Create two more clones from the master star. If you have several clones and you aren't sure which object is the master, select one of the clones, and then click **Select Master** on the **Select** menu.

The master is selected along with the clone.

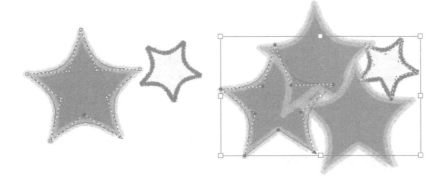

If you delete the master, the clones will remain on the page and one of the clones will become the new master.

CLOSE the *paths_and_clones.design* file without saving any changes.

> **Tip** You cannot create a clone of a text object unless you first convert the text to paths, but the text would no longer be editable.
>
> You can break the link of a clone to its master by selecting the clone, and then on the Object menu, clicking Convert Object To Path. This turns the clone into an editable object.

Creating and Saving Custom Strokes

Strokes are at the heart of what makes Expression Design special. Not only can you use the strokes that come with the program, you can create and save custom strokes. Custom strokes can be created from any object or group of vector objects, from strokes in the Strokes Gallery, and even from bitmap images.

Creating and Saving Vector Strokes

In this exercise, you will use objects drawn in Expression Design to create a custom vector stroke, which you will then save for future use.

> **USE** the *save_stroke.design* file. This practice file is located in the *Documents\Microsoft Press\Expression Design SBS\UsingStrokes* folder.
>
> **OPEN** the *save_stroke.design* file.

1. A stroke can be created from one object or multiple objects. The practice file has two objects you will select together and save as one stroke. On the **Select** menu, click **All** to select both objects.

> **Tip** The darker the artwork is, the brighter the stroke will be. Black areas of the artwork will result in vibrant areas on the final stroke.

2. On the **Object** menu, click **Stroke**, and then click **New Stroke Definition**. Any fill or stroke on the paths of the object or objects will become part of the stroke.

In the stroke definition window, a red box is displayed around the stroke artwork. This is the *stroke definition box*, which defines the area that will be included in the stroke. Notice that there is an arrow in the center of the box. This indicates the direction your stroke will follow when it is applied to a path. Notice also that there is empty space between the artwork and the stroke definition box. You can remove this excess space to keep the final brush stroke from being too spaced out.

> **Tip** Notice that the stroke definition gets the default name of *NoName*.

Stroke
Definition Box

3. At the bottom of the Toolbox are three new tools that are visible only when the stroke definition window is active. Click the **Stroke Definition Box** tool and then drag a new outline around the stroke artwork to get rid of the excess space.

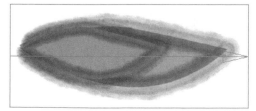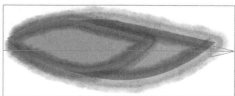

> **Tip**   If you have a hard time dragging the new outline, try turning off the Snap To
> Guides feature.

4. On the **File** menu, click **Save** to save the stroke. This will make a basic brush that
flows along the path, stretching to fit. In the dialog box, type a name for your
brush and choose a **Strokes Gallery** folder in the menu. I left mine in the **General**
category. Click **OK** to save the brush to the **Strokes Gallery**.

The brush is now in the Strokes Gallery as the active brush and can be applied to
a path.

5. Open a new document window 800 pixels wide by 600 pixels high at a resolution
of 96 pixels per inch, and draw an open path with the **Paintbrush**. The new brush
should be the active brush stroke in the **Strokes Gallery**, but if it isn't, scroll until
you find it, and click it to apply it to the path you draw.

6. In the **Color Picker**, change the stroke color, and adjust the width of the stroke if
necessary. Try drawing an ellipse to evaluate how your brush fits the path.

7. Notice the gap at the top of the ellipse. This may indicate that your stroke definition includes too much extra space. You can fix this by editing the stroke. On the
Object menu, click **Stroke**, and then click **Edit Stroke Definition** to open the stroke
definition work area again. Use the **Stroke Definition Box** tool to draw a new
boundary that falls within the front and back edges of the brush.

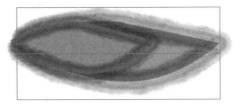

8. Save the brush again. The **Save** dialog box will have the brush name already entered; click **OK** to accept the name and, when asked if you want to overwrite the original brush, click **Yes**.

9. Click the **Flip** tab on the flip bar to open the document to which you applied the stroke after the first save.

Notice in ours that the brush stroke has updated, and the ellipse no longer has the space.

10. Brush strokes can also be made to repeat rather than stretch along the path. On the **Object** menu, click **Stroke**, and then click **Edit Stroke Definition** to open the stroke definition window again.

11. On the **Select** menu, click **All**.

12. Right-click the image to open the context menu, and choose **Make Repeating**. You can drag the repeat handles to change the area that will be repeated, but for this brush stroke the default will work quite nicely. On the **File** menu, click **Save**, and this time, give the brush stroke a new name. We called ours *my_brush2*.

13. Draw a new path on your test document and apply the new brush. Notice how the design repeats. You may need to adjust the width of the stroke to fit the size of your path.

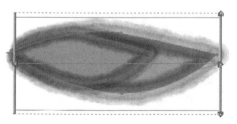

✕ **CLOSE** the *save_stroke.design* file without saving any changes.

Anchoring Strokes

Some brushes would look odd if repeated or stretched along the path. For these, you can anchor part of the artwork so only part of it stretches. An example is a brush made up of a hand and arm. If you were to define the hand and arm as a plain stroke, the hand would be distorted from being stretched along the path, as is shown in the following example.

In this exercise, you will anchor part of the artwork so only part of it stretches along the path.

USE the *hand.design* file. This practice file is located in the *Documents\Microsoft Press\ Expression Design SBS\UsingStrokes* folder.
OPEN the *hand.design* file.

Selection

Stroke
Definition Box

Direct Selection

Stroke
Anchor Point

1. With the **Selection** tool, select the hand and arm. On the **Object** menu, click **Stroke**, and then click **New Stroke Definition**.

2. In the stroke definition window, use the **Stroke Definition Box** tool to refine the area for the stroke.

3. Drag the **Direct Selection** tool around the wrist and hand to select only those anchor points. Selected anchor points will be solid red.

4. Right-click the arm and, from the context menu, choose **Anchor To End**. A small anchor will display at the end of the hand. The Anchor Tool is now the active tool in the Toolbox. You can use this tool to reposition the anchor at the end of the hand if needed. The selected anchor points will be anchored to the end of the stroke and will not be distorted when the stroke is used.

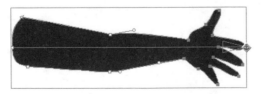

5. Save the stroke as **arm**. On your test image, use the **Paintbrush** tool to draw a line. Notice that the hand stays at the end of the path.

You can change the color of the arm and adjust the width. If you use the Pen tool, you can add a hard elbow joint to the arm (not just bendy curve points) by clicking at the shoulder to start the arm, clicking at the elbow to add the joint, and double-clicking where you want the hand to end the stroke.

CLOSE the *hand.design* file without saving any changes.

Creating Strokes from Images

Bitmap strokes are created from images. These strokes can be found in the Strokes Gallery in the Photos category, although they do not have to be photos.

In this exercise, you will save an image stroke from a .png file.

USE the *redrose.png* file. This practice file is located in the *Documents\Microsoft Press\ Expression Design SBS\UsingStrokes* folder.

1. Start a new image 800 pixels wide by 600 pixels high at 96 pixels per inch.

2. On the **File** menu, click **Import**, and navigate to the *Documents\Microsoft Press\ Expression Design SBS\UsingStrokes* folder. Double-click *redrose.png* to open it in Expression Design.

   To make an image stroke, you need to use a format that supports transparency to keep from having a white background on the final stroke. The file used here is a rose like the one you worked on in Chapter 6, exported and saved as a transparent .png file in Photoshop CS3. (You will learn about exporting your work in Chapter 10, "Exporting and Printing Your Work.")

3. Ensure that the rose is selected. On the **Object** menu, click **Stroke**, and then click **Define Image Stroke.** The Define Image Stroke dialog box opens.

4. Name the brush **Red Rose**, and choose the **Photos** folder as the location of the brush. For **Alpha Channel**, choose **Use original alpha value.** Leave the default width.

5. In the **Body Section** box, choose **Simple Repeat.** Leave the **Anchor head and tail sections** lengths set at 0 pixels. Click **OK** to save the brush.

6. Try the new image brush on several different paths. Adjust the width of the stroke to fit the length of the path.

Repeating Petals for Floral Fun

Try drawing a petal and creating a repeating stroke. When applied to a straight line, the stroke isn't terribly impressive.

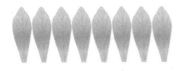

However, when applied to a series of circles decreasing in size, each rotated slightly, it's a fast way to make a chrysanthemum. Apply the stroke to two circles, rotate the inner circle slightly, add a center, and you have a sunflower.

Using the Blend Paths Command

The Blend Paths command takes two or more paths and creates a series of intermediate paths between them, based on object shapes and attributes. The number of steps you choose determines how smoothly the objects blend. In the following image, the original two circles on the left were blended with a linear blend. The center blend has 3 steps, and the blend on the right has 15 steps.

Expression Design uses one of two methods to interpolate the blend when you select two objects to blend. In the Blend Paths dialog box, there are two choices: Linear Interpolate and Angle And Length Interpolate. These two options differ in the way they treat the anchor points on the source paths when making the blend, as illustrated in the following two images.

- **Linear Interpolate.** When you use this method, Expression Design treats all anchor points on the path as individual anchor points with no regard to the existence or position of other anchor points on the path. The petals on the left in the illustration were blended with eight steps, using linear interpolation. Notice that the tops of the petals are even.

- **Angle And Length Interpolate.** When you use this method, Expression Design takes into account the angle and length between anchor points when making the blend. In the image on the right, the same two petals were blended with eight steps, using angle and length interpolation, and the petals arch across the top. The steps between the individual blended paths are called *in-betweens*.

In this exercise on the following page, you will blend several objects together, using the two different interpolation methods to accomplish blended paths.

> **USE** the *blends.design* file. This practice file is located in the *Documents\Microsoft Press\Expression Design SBS\UsingStrokes* folder.
>
> **OPEN** the *blends.design* file.

Selection

1. With the **Selection** tool, select the two lines on the left side of the document window.

2. On the **Object** menu, click **Blend Paths**. In the **Blend Paths** dialog box, enter **10** for the steps and choose **Linear** for the interpolation.

3. Click **OK**. There should now be a blend in which the colors have blended and the low number of steps shows each in-between on the blend.

4. With the **Selection** tool, select the two lines on the right side of the document window. On the **Object** menu, click **Blend Paths**. In the **Blend Paths** dialog box, enter **30** for the steps and choose **Angle and Length** for the interpolation.

5. Click **OK**. The blend is much smoother, and the angle and length interpolation has added a curve to the blend, a more natural progression than linear.

6. Using blends is a good way to create the illusion of contours. Use the **Selection** tool to select the circle.

7. On the **Edit** menu, click **Copy**, and then click **Paste in Front** to place the copy directly on top of the original. Be very careful not to click the page and accidentally deselect the copy!

8. In the favorites on the **Color Picker**, click the **Stroke** tab, and then click the bright yellow swatch to change the color of the copy's stroke to yellow.

Options

9. In the Action Bar at the bottom of the window, open the **Options** menu and ensure that **Scale As Percentage** is selected.

10. Type **90%** in the **Width** box, and then press Enter. The **Height** box measurement should also change to 90 percent. If it doesn't, you will have to type **90** in the **Height** box, too, and press Enter.

This will scale the yellow copy of the circle to 90 percent of the size of the original orange circle, and will also keep the second circle centered inside the first.

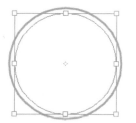

11. With the yellow circle still selected, on the **Edit** menu, click **Copy**, and then click **Paste in Front** to place the second copy directly on top of the first copy. Being careful not to deselect the copy, click the orange color swatch in the favorites in the **Color Picker** to change this circle's stroke color.

12. Once again, on the Action Bar, type **80%** in the **Width** box, and press Enter. The **Height** box measurement should also change to **80%**. If it doesn't, you will have to type **80%** in the **Height** box, too, and press Enter.

This will scale the smaller orange circle to 80 percent of the size of the original circle and center the third circle inside the second.

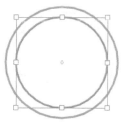

> **Tip** Expression Design keeps track of the transformation of an object for as long as that object exists, which makes it incredibly easy for you to undo the entire sequence of transformations and revert to the original shape of the path at any time in the future—even after you've saved, closed, and reopened the document window! (That little feature mystified our technical editor.) To undo all transformations on an object, select the object, point to Transform on the Arrange menu, and then click Reset Transform. To make all transformations permanent—that is, to force Expression Design to forget the object's transformation information—select the object, and click Reset Bounding Box under Transform on the Arrange menu.

13. Select all three circles, and then on the **Object** menu, click **Blend Paths**. Set the number of steps to 15, and choose **Linear** for the interpolation. Click **OK**.

There should now be a gold ring with a nice three-dimensional look.

14. Now make a pair of interlocking rings. Select all of the ring pieces (17 total, after blending), and on the **Arrange** menu, click **Group**. On the **Edit** menu, click **Copy**, and then click **Paste**. Overlap the two rings as shown in the following image.

15. On the **Edit** menu, click **Paste** again to add a third ring to the document. Drag it away from the two rings you have overlapped. In order to create the illusion that the rings are interlocking, you'll have to cover up one of the areas where the top ring is crossing over the bottom ring.

16. You need a piece to put over the area where the top ring crosses the bottom. In order to get the piece, you'll make a clipper. On the extra ring, drag a square with no fill on top of it, corresponding with the area that you need to cover, as in the image on the left below.

None

17. The stroke is needed for placement only, so as soon as you position it where you want the clipper, remove the stroke from the square. Make sure both the rectangle and the entire extra ring are selected, as shown on the right in the image below.

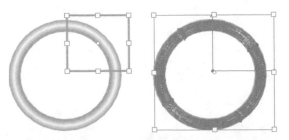

18. On the **Object** menu, click **Clipping Path**, and then click **Make With Top Path**. Deselect the current selection. Your screen will look like the image on the left in the illustration at the end of this exercise.

19. Drag the clipped section on top of the top overlapped ring.

> **Tip** Remember that you can use the Arrow keys to nudge the ring into place.

20. Select all of the ring pieces, and on the **Arrange** menu, click **Group** to keep them together. Then deselect the objects to display the result.

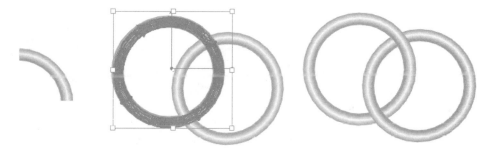

> **CLOSE** the *blends.design* file without saving any changes. If you are not continuing directly to the next chapter, exit Expression Design.

Key Points

- Strokes can be added to any path created in Expression Design.
- You can add natural media strokes to simulate watercolor and other kinds of media.
- When you create your own custom brush strokes from vector paths or bitmap images, you can create unique images.
- The Blend Paths command takes two or more paths and creates a series of intermediate paths between them based on object shapes and attributes.
- You can use clipping paths to make objects look interlinked.

Chapter at a Glance

Set style attributes for text, **page 175**

Set advanced text attributes, **page 181**

Put text in a path, **page 189**

8 Working with Text

In this chapter, you will learn to:

✔ Create text objects.

✔ Set style attributes for text.

✔ Set advanced text attributes.

✔ Put text on a path.

✔ Put text in a path.

✔ Convert text to paths.

A picture might be worth a thousand words, but sometimes not even that many are enough. Charts and graphs require captions. Flowcharts and diagrams call for labels. Interface designs need button text. Even cartoons benefit from word balloons. No matter how visual graphic design intends to be, it relies on the assistance of the written word perhaps more often than it would like to admit.

In this chapter, you will learn how to incorporate text into your Microsoft Expression Design documents. You will edit the text's appearance attributes as well as its content. You will attach it to paths in two different ways, and you will convert it from text into standard vector graphics to increase its usefulness as a purely visual element.

Important Before you can use the practice files in this chapter, you need to install them from the book's companion CD to their default location. See "Using the Book's CD" at the beginning of this book for more information.

Troubleshooting Graphics and operating system–related instructions in this book reflect the Windows Vista user interface. If your computer is running Windows XP and you experience trouble following the instructions as written, please refer to the "Information for Readers Running Windows XP" section at the beginning of this book.

Creating Text Objects

A text object is a special kind of vector graphic that contains typographical characters, or *glyphs*, which are similar (but not identical) to closed paths. Each glyph in a **text object** can have its own stroke and fill attributes, and although you cannot apply effects to each glyph individually, you *can* apply effects to the text object as a whole. And because the glyphs are like vectors, you can stretch them, scale them, and otherwise transform them without any loss of image quality.

> **Tip** When you select a text object, a bounding box with handles appears around it. Drag the handles to *scale* or stretch the text object; drag one of the corner handles to rotate the text object; drag one of the side handles to *skew* the text object; or use any of the commands on the Arrange menu, under Transform, to alter the text object in various ways.
>
>

But what really sets text objects apart is that the glyphs remain editable as text, not as graphics. If you misspell a word, you don't have to redraw it by using the Paintbrush or the Pen tool; you simply retype it. You can change the font, style, size, and alignment properties of the text as well as its wording and spelling at any stage of production.

In this exercise, you will create and edit text objects.

> **USE** the *barchart.design* file. This practice file is located in the *Documents\Microsoft Press\ Expression Design SBS\WorkingText* folder.
>
> **BE SURE TO** start Expression Design before beginning this exercise.
>
> **OPEN** the *barchart.design* file.

1. Study the bar chart that is displayed. The illustration consists of separate layers for the grid and bar elements; these layers are locked.

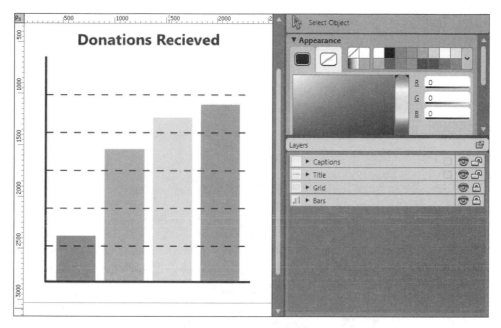

There is also a layer for the title of the chart. The title itself is a text object that contains a spelling mistake. The text should read "Donations Received." You will correct the spelling later in this exercise.

The topmost layer—Captions—is currently empty. You will add text objects to this layer as labels for the bars in the chart. The illustration includes a guide rule near the bottom so that you'll know exactly where to create the text objects.

> **Tip** You might need to adjust the zoom level of the document window to 75% to see the guide rule.

2. In the **Layers** panel, click the **Captions** layer to select it.

3. In the Toolbox, click the **Text** tool.

4. Point to the document window.

Text

I-beam

The pointer takes the form of an I-beam with a short horizontal line near the bottom. This line marks the *baseline* of the text, or the standard bottom position of the glyphs. The baseline is like the rule on a piece of notebook paper. Letters such as the lowercase *a* and *e* rest entirely on top of the baseline, whereas letters such as the lowercase *p* and *q* have *descenders* that dip below the baseline a short distance.

5. Position the pointer underneath the leftmost bar in the chart—the red bar—so that the baseline marker touches the guide rule.

6. Click the mouse button.

Expression Design inserts a flashing cursor.

7. Type the caption: **2005**.

The chart starts with the year 2005. As you type, Expression Design adds the glyphs for the numbers to the new text object that you created.

8. Press Esc, or hold down Ctrl and click a blank area of the document window.

Expression Design "closes" the text object. However, you are free to edit it at any time.

> **Tip** Don't press Enter to escape from the text object. The Enter key works just as it does in a word processing program; it starts a new line.

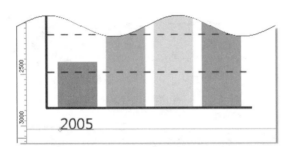

9. Repeat steps 5 through 8 for each of the bars in the graph. Make captions for the years 2006, 2007, and 2008.

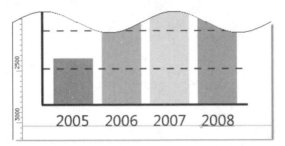

10. In the **Layers** panel, click the **Title** layer to select it.

11. Point to the **i** and **e** in the misspelled word **Recieved**.

I-beam Brackets

Expression Design encloses the I-beam in brackets, which signifies that clicking will edit the existing text instead of creating a new text object.

12. Drag around the **i** and the **e** to select them.

Expression Design highlights this string of letters.

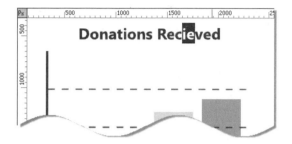

13. Type **e** and **i** to correct the spelling.

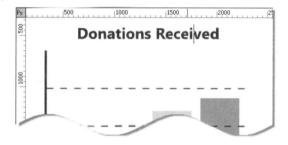

14. Press ⌫Esc, or hold down ⌃Ctrl and click a blank area of the document window.

Expression Design "closes" the text object with your edits intact. Your bar chart is now ready to save or print.

CLOSE the *barchart.design* file without saving any changes.

Setting Style Attributes for Text

As mentioned previously, with Expression Design, you can set many different style attributes for text objects. Most of these attributes can apply either to individual glyphs within the text object or to the text object as a whole—whichever makes more sense for your particular needs. Other attributes apply only to the text object as a whole; you cannot use them on individual glyphs.

> **Tip** Expression Design applies style attributes differently depending on your selection. If you use the Text tool to select an individual glyph or a string of glyphs, Expression Design applies the attributes to those characters only. If you use the Selection tool to select the text object as a whole, Expression Design applies the attributes to all the glyphs in the text object.

You specify the style attributes of text objects in the Properties panel, under the Appearance category:

- **Fill.** The fill color represents the basic color of the text. It's the color of the "body" of the letters and numbers. Each individual glyph can have its own fill attribute, or you can apply the fill to the entire text object.

- **Stroke.** The stroke is displayed as an outline around the letters and numbers. By default, the glyphs in a text object have a stroke of None, but you are free to specify a stroke color, stroke style, and stroke width of your choosing. Each individual glyph can have its own stroke attributes, or you can apply them to the entire text object.

- **Opacity.** The opacity of the stroke and fill work exactly the same for text objects as they do for other types of vector graphics. You can set the opacity levels for individual glyphs, or you can set them for the entire text object.

- **Advanced appearance attributes.** The Blend Mode, Fill Rule, Joint, Caps, and Dash settings all apply to text objects just as they do to other types of vector graphics, and you can set them for individual glyphs or the entire text object. To see them, click the Show Advanced Properties button.

> **Tip** You can set style attributes for the text object before you actually type the text. To do so, click the Text tool in the Toolbox, but do not create a text object just yet. Adjust the attributes in the Properties panel as you want, and then click to create the text object. This trick works with text attributes only; attributes in the Appearance category revert to their defaults when you create the text object.

The special typographical attributes of text objects are in the Text category of the Properties panel:

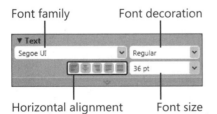

Font family   Font decoration

Horizontal alignment   Font size

- **Font family.** The *font family* setting determines the typeface of the text. You can set the font for each glyph individually, or you can set it for the entire text object.

- **Font decoration.** The *font decoration* setting determines the typographical style of the text: regular, boldface, italic, and so on. Exactly which font decorations are available to you depends on your choice for the font family. Not all fonts support an italic style, for instance. You can set the font decoration for each glyph individually, or you can set it for the entire text object.

- **Horizontal alignment.** The *horizontal alignment* buttons determine how Expression Design positions the lines of the text in the text object:

    - **Align Left.** Expression Design positions all the lines on the left margin of the text object.

    - **Align Center.** Expression Design centers all the lines horizontally within the width of the text object.

    - **Align Right.** Expression Design positions all the lines on the right margin of the text object.

    - **Justify.** In all but the last line of a paragraph, Expression Design inserts space as padding between words, so that all the affected lines have the same length.

    - **Justify All.** In every line of a paragraph, including the last line, Expression Design inserts space as padding between words, so that all the lines in the text object have the same length.

> **Tip** The Justify and Justify All alignment settings apply to area text only. See the "Putting Text in a Path" section later in this chapter for more information on area text.

Your choice of alignment setting applies to the entire text object. Individual lines or glyphs cannot have separate alignments. Therefore, if you want to center the first line of a text object but keep the rest of the lines aligned on the left, you need two separate text objects: one for the centered line and one for the left-aligned lines.

- **Type size.** The *type size* setting determines the overall dimensions of the glyphs. You can set the type size for each glyph individually, or you can set it for the entire text object.

> **Tip** Advanced text attributes such as leading and tracking are discussed in the next section.

You add effects to text objects under the Effects category of the Properties panel, just as you would for other types of vectors. Although you can apply effects to the text object as a whole, you cannot apply them to individual glyphs.

> **Tip** If you need to apply different effects to different glyphs, you can always convert a text object into ordinary vector paths. You lose the ability to edit the text as text, but you gain complete control over the paths as graphical elements. For more information, see the "Converting Text to Paths" section later in this chapter.

In this exercise, you will set basic style attributes for individual glyphs as well as entire text objects.

> **USE** the *abc.design* file. This practice file is located in the *Documents\Microsoft Press\ Expression Design SBS\WorkingText* folder.
>
> **OPEN** the *abc.design* file.

1. Look at the design. It consists of one layer with two unstyled text objects. For convenience, we'll call them the **ABC** and **XYZ** objects.

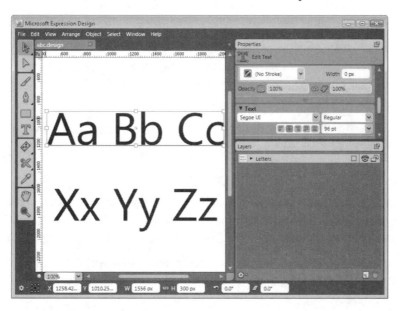

Selection

2. In the Toolbox, click the **Selection** tool.

3. Click the **ABC** object to select it.

4. In the **Properties** panel, expand the **Text** category.

   Note the current attributes of the text object: It's set in the Segoe UI font family with regular styling at 96 points, and its alignment is centered.

5. On the **Font Family** menu, click **Times New Roman**.

   Because you selected the text object as a whole with the Selection tool, Expression Design applied this attribute to all the glyphs in the text object.

6. Now select the **XYZ** text object, and set its font family to **Arial**.

   The typeface of the text changes accordingly.

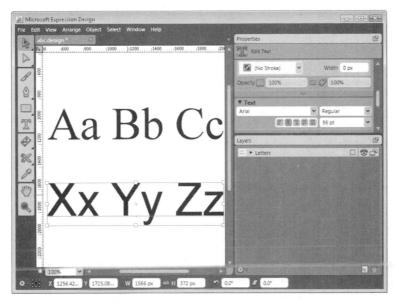

Text

7. In the Toolbox, click the **Text** tool.

8. Select the lowercase **a** in the **ABC** text object by dragging across this glyph.

Expression Design highlights the lowercase *a*.

9. On the **Font Decoration** menu, click **Italic**.

Expression Design sets the style of the lowercase *a* to italic without affecting the other glyphs in the text object.

10. By the same procedure, change the lowercase **b** and the lowercase **c** to italic style.

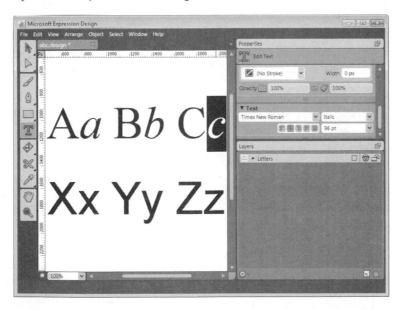

11. Select the uppercase **X** in the **XYZ** text object.

Expression Design highlights this glyph.

12. In the **Properties** panel, expand the **Appearance** category.

13. Set the fill of the glyph to red (**R255, G0, B0**).

Expression Design changes the color of the uppercase *X* from black to red.

14. Set the stroke of the glyph to black (**R0, G0, B0**) with a width of **8** pixels.

Expression Design outlines the uppercase *X* in black.

15. By the same procedure, change the colors of the uppercase **Y** and **Z** to green (**R100, G255, B0**) and blue (**R0, G150, B255**), respectively, and apply black, 8-pixel strokes to each.

> **Tip** As you work, feel free to experiment with other style attributes.

Your exercise is now ready to save or print.

CLOSE the *abc.design* file without saving any changes.

Setting Advanced Text Attributes

Additional text attributes appear in the Text category of the Properties panel when you click the Show Advanced Properties button:

- **Leading.** The *Leading* setting controls the amount of space between lines of type in a text object. (Remember that you can create a multi-line text object by pressing Enter.) The default value, Auto, automatically determines the leading based on the type size of the text. A value of 100 percent is roughly equivalent to automatic leading. Anything less than 100 percent decreases the usual amount of space between the lines, while anything more than 100 percent increases the usual amount of space.

> **Tip** The term *leading* is a holdover from the days of manual typesetting. Typographers used to increase line spacing by physically inserting lead plugs between the lines.

  You can apply leading to one or more lines of type by selecting the lines with the Text tool, or you can apply it to the text object as a whole.

- **Tracking.** The *Tracking* setting controls the amount of space between two or more glyphs. The default value, 0 percent, indicates standard tracking. Any value less than 0 percent decreases the usual amount of spacing, making it tighter, while any value greater than 0 percent increases the usual amount of spacing, making it looser.

  You can apply tracking to individual glyphs or to the entire text object, although it is almost always used on a case-by-case basis. When you apply it individually, you should always focus on the glyph on the left side of the spacing problem. For instance, if the *t* and the *h* **collide** or superimpose each other in the word *theory*, you'll want to increase the tracking of the *t* glyph, because the *t* is to the left of the *h*. Likewise, if the *i* and the *l* are too far apart in the word *pile*, decrease the tracking of the *i* glyph, because the *i* is to the left of the *l*.

- **Horizontal scale.** The *horizontal scale* setting determines the relative width of a glyph. The default value is 100 percent. Anything lower makes the glyph narrower than usual, and anything higher makes it wider than usual. You can apply the horizontal scale to individual glyphs, or you can set it for the entire text object.

- **Baseline offset.** The *baseline offset* setting determines where Expression Design sets the glyph in relation to the baseline of the line of type. A positive offset raises the text above the baseline, and a negative offset drops the text below the baseline. You can apply the baseline offset to individual glyphs, or you can set it for the entire text object.

- **Script.** The *script* setting lets you create *subscripts*, or smaller glyphs that descend below the baseline; and *superscripts*, or smaller glyphs that rise above the baseline. The regular setting displays the glyphs normally. You can apply the script attribute to individual glyphs, or you can set it for the entire text object.

In this exercise, you will set advanced text attributes for individual glyphs as well as entire text objects. (You will also discover how to acquire a little vending-machine money by kidnapping your co-worker's action figure collection.)

> **USE** the *ransom.design* file. This practice file is located in the *Documents\Microsoft Press\ Expression Design SBS\WorkingText* folder.
>
> **OPEN** the *ransom.design* file.

1. Look at the ransom note. It consists of one layer with a multi-line text object that includes many different font families.

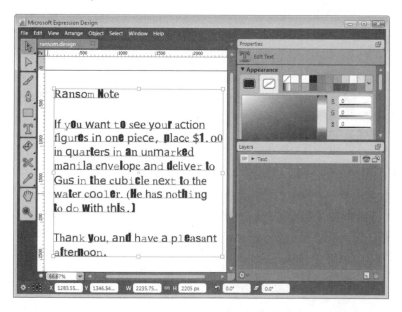

Selection

2. In the Toolbox, click the **Selection** tool.

3. Click the text object to select it.

4. In the **Properties** panel, expand the **Text** category, and click the **Show Advanced Properties** button.

5. On the **Leading** menu, click **125%**.

Expression Design increases the amount of space between each line, which makes your ransom note easier to read.

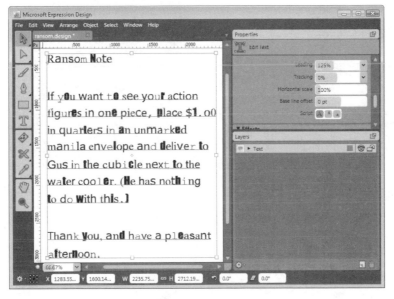

Text

6. In the Toolbox, click the **Text** tool.

Notice how the *f* collides with the *i*. This is not uncommon when two font families are side by side in the same word. We'll fix this problem by adjusting the tracking of the *f*.

> **Tip** Typographical collisions look unprofessional and should always be corrected.

7. At the beginning of the second line of the ransom note, drag to select the lowercase **f** in the word **figures**.

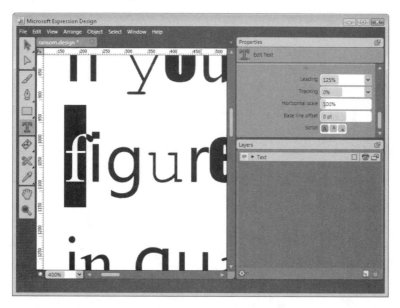

8. In the **Properties** panel, in the advanced options, click **10%** on the **Tracking** menu.

Expression Design tracks the *f* glyph a little looser than usual, which prevents the
collision with the *i* glyph.

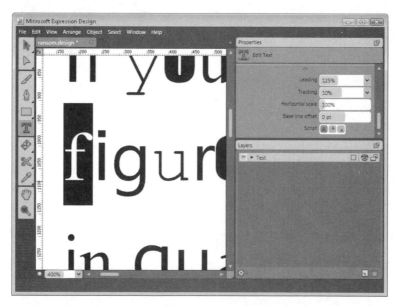

9. Use the same procedure to set the tracking of the lowercase **r** in the word **figures**
to **5%** to prevent its near-collision with the **e** glyph.

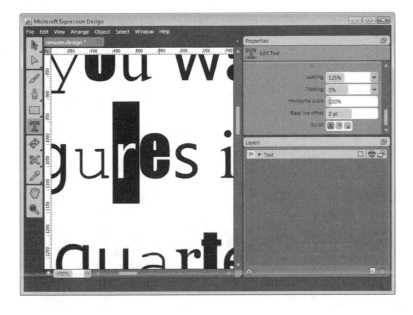

Tip Even when glyphs don't actually collide, the tracking might feel too tight or too loose in certain places. Use your own good judgment to decide when to decrease or increase the character spacing.

Your ransom note is now ready to save or print.

CLOSE the *ransom.design* file without saving any changes.

Putting Text on a Path

When you create a new text object, Expression Design includes a baseline by default. However, if you want, you can attach the text to a baseline of your own—an existing vector graphic. Your text follows the contour of the path for a variety of uses and effects.

In this exercise, you will attach text to a path.

USE the *valentine.design* file. This practice file is located in the *Documents\Microsoft Press\Expression Design SBS\WorkingText* folder.

BE SURE TO reset the active workspace before beginning this exercise.

OPEN the *valentine.design* file.

1. Study the valentine illustration. This illustration consists of two layers: **Heart (outline)**, which contains a heart with a black stroke and no fill; and **Heart (filled)**, which contains an identical heart shape with no stroke and a solid red fill.

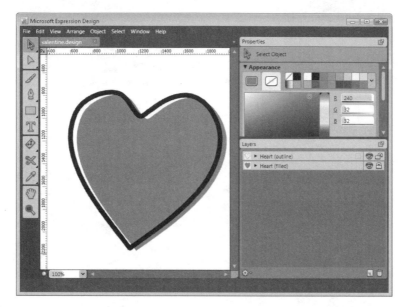

2. In the **Layers** panel, click the **Heart (outline)** layer to select it.

   You will attach the text to the path on this layer. Note that the *Heart (filled)* layer is locked to prevent you from accidentally attaching the text to the path on that layer instead.

   > **Tip** When you have two or more overlapping objects in very close proximity, it's not always easy to tell which one Expression Design is indicating. For this reason, you might want to separate the object that you plan to modify by placing it on a layer of its own and then locking the other layer or layers, at least temporarily. This way, there is no question about which object you're editing, so you don't have to spend time thinking about it.

Text

3. In the Toolbox, click the **Text** tool.

4. In the **Properties** panel, expand the **Text** category, and set the following text-specific attributes of the tool:

   - On the **Font Family** menu, click **Georgia**.
   - On the **Font Decoration** menu, click **Italic**.
   - Click the **Align Left** button.

Align Left

   - On the **Type Size** menu, click **24 pt**.

> **Tip** Think of the initial attributes as a starting point and nothing more. You can always fine-tune them after you view the results.

5. Point to the path.

Text On Path

The small horizontal line on the pointer changes into a longer wavy line to indicate that the text will flow along this path.

> **Tip** It doesn't matter so much where exactly you point, as long as it is somewhere along the path. You will finalize the placement of the text in a later step.

6. Click the mouse button.

Expression Design displays a flashing cursor at the position on the path that you chose in step 5.

> **Tip** To attach a text object you have already created to the path, select both the text object and the path, and then on the Object menu, point to Text On Path, and click Attach Text. If you placed the text object inside a path, click Attach Area Text instead. For more information about area text, see "Putting Text in a Path," later in this chapter.

7. Type the text: **Dearest Melinda, I love you! ~ Bill.**

Expression Design adds the text to the selected layer and causes it to flow along the path.

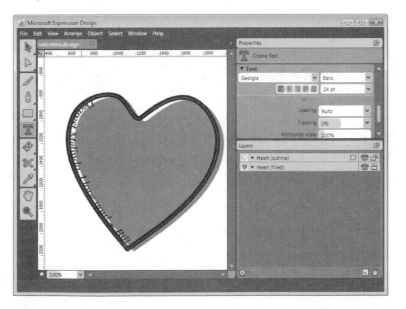

> **Tip** Remember that paths have a direction. When you attach text to a path, the text proceeds toward the path's ending point. To change the direction in which the text flows, change the direction of the path by selecting the path, and then clicking Reverse Path on the Object menu.

Notice that the baseline of the text matches the path exactly. Because the path is relatively heavy, and because both the path and the text are black, the letters are not entirely visible. One solution to this particular problem is to adjust the baseline offset of the text.

Selection

8. In the Toolbox, click the **Selection** tool. If Expression Design doesn't automatically select the text object, point to the text, and then click.

9. In the **Properties** panel, under the **Text** category, click the **Show Advanced Properties** button (if they are not already visible). Locate the **Base line offset** control, and set the baseline offset to **-24 pt**.

Expression Design moves the text 24 points beneath the baseline (and therefore 24 points beneath the path).

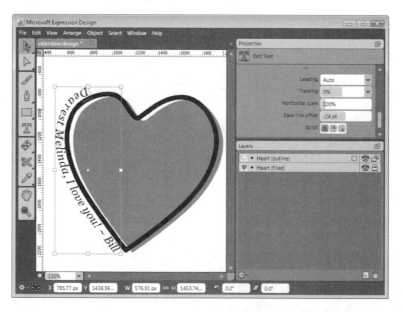

> **Tip** Remember, a negative baseline offset positions the text below the baseline, and a positive baseline offset positions the text above the baseline.

10. While the text object is selected and the **Selection** tool is active, point to the perpendicular line at the beginning of the text object. The pointer changes into an I-beam with an arrow on either side.

> **Tip** To detach the text from the path, click the text object with the Selection tool and, on the Object menu, point to Text On Path, and then click Release Text.

11. Drag to position the text exactly where you want it along the path.

> **Tip** You must switch to one of the selection tools to move the text; the Text tool doesn't have this functionality. However, any selection tool will work, not just the black arrow.

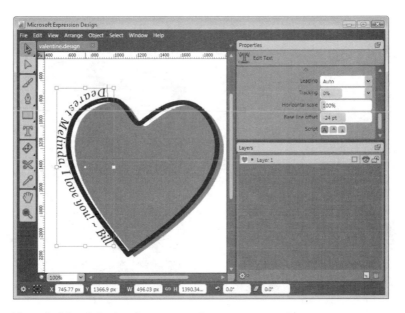

Your finished design is now ready to save or print.

✖ **CLOSE** the *valentine.design* file without saving any changes.

Putting Text in a Path

We have mentioned area text a couple of times in passing without providing much in the way of an explanation. Simply enough, *area text* is text that displays inside a path. Think of the path as a kind of container for the text. Area text does not replace the path's fill (if one is specified); in fact, the fill is completely unaffected by whatever area text may share the interior of the object.

> **Tip** An open path can hold area text, but the effects are not always reliable. For best results, use closed paths as containers for area text, or use open paths with well-defined interior regions.

In this exercise, you will create area text.

USE the *wordballoon.design* file. This practice file is located in the *Documents\Microsoft Press\Expression Design SBS\WorkingText* folder.

OPEN the *wordballoon.design* file.

1. Look at the illustration of the word balloon. It consists of one layer—**Word balloon**—that contains one closed path with a drop shadow effect.

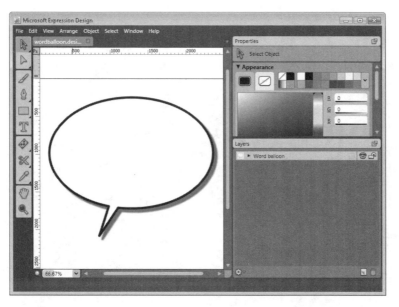

2. In the Toolbox, click the **Text** tool.

Text

3. In the **Properties** panel, expand the **Text** category, and then set the following text-specific attributes of the object:

- On the **Font Family** menu, click **Comic Sans MS**.

- On the **Font Decoration** menu, click **Regular**.

- Click the **Align Center** button.

Align Center

- On the **Type Size** menu, click **48 pt**.

Tip You specified a baseline offset in the previous exercise, and Expression Design might still "remember" this setting. So in the advanced properties, make sure that the value of the Base Line Offset control is 0 pt.

4. Point to the interior of the word **balloon**, and then hold down the ⬚Shift⬚ key.

Text in Path

A closed-path shape displays around the pointer, indicating that Expression Design will use the path as the container of the text.

> **Tip** It so happens that the word *balloon* has a white fill, so you can point inside the object to place the text. When the desired object doesn't have a fill, you must point to its stroke. Be careful, though! If you don't hold down the Shift key, Expression Design assumes that you want to place the text *on* the path, not *in* the path. Keep your eye on the pointer to be sure of what Expression Design intends to do when you click the mouse button.

5. Click the mouse button, and then release the ⎡Shift⎤ key.

Expression Design inserts a flashing cursor inside the word balloon.

6. Turn on ⎡Caps Lock⎤, and type the text: **WE SAVED THE WALLACE ACCOUNT! ASK ME HOW.**

Expression Design fills the path with the text.

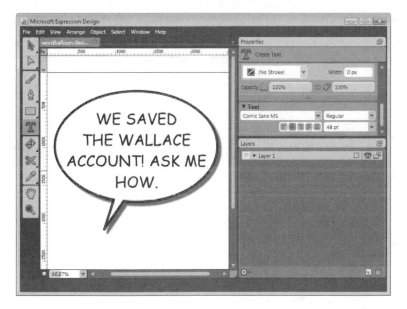

> **Tip** To detach the text from the inside of the path, click the text object with the Selection tool; then on the Object menu, point to Text On Path, and click Release Text.

7. Turn off ⎡Caps Lock⎤.

Your finished design is now ready to save or print.

CLOSE the *wordballoon.design* file without saving any changes.

Converting Text to Paths

You know from the beginning of this chapter that text objects, though very similar to vector graphics, are not entirely equivalent. You lose a bit of flexibility in editing the glyphs as graphics, but you gain a great many conveniences in editing the glyphs as text.

Sometimes, though, the limitations of text objects outweigh the benefits. If, for example, you need to apply different effects to different glyphs in the same text object, you cannot proceed with text objects alone. You might also need to edit the shape or construction of the glyphs themselves beyond what the standard style attributes provide you. In short, you might need to treat the glyphs as visual elements in your design, not as letters, numbers, and punctuation marks.

In cases such as these, you can convert any text object into a visually identical group of vector paths. These paths look exactly as they did in glyph form, so to a human, they read exactly the same; however, as far as Expression Design is concerned, the letters and numbers are no longer glyphs. They are merely glyph-shaped vector graphics. The Text tool has no effect on them, so you cannot edit their content, style, or spelling—but you *can* modify their construction whenever you want by using any vector-editing tool or menu command.

> **Tip** Because you lose text-editing capability when you convert a text object into a path, be sure that the style and content of your text is exactly as you want it before you convert. For similar reasons, it's never a bad idea to save a version of your document with the unconverted text object in place. That way, you don't have to recreate the text object from scratch if you find a spelling error or if you decide to change the wording.

In this exercise, you will convert a text object into a group of paths and then alter the structure of one of the letters.

USE the *smile.design* and *smile_dot.design* files. These practice files are located in the *Documents\Microsoft Press\Expression Design SBS\WorkingText* folder.

OPEN the *smile.design* and *smile_dot.design* files. (To open both files at the same time, hold down Ctrl, select both files, and then click Open.)

1. Look at the document window, with the two tabs at the top. The *smile.design* file contains the main design for a mini-poster, and *smile_dot.design* contains a custom-designed dot for the letter **i** in the word **smile**.

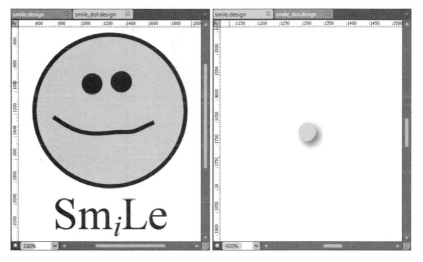

2. Switch to the *smile.design* document window by clicking its flip tab in the flip bar at the top of the window.

3. In the Toolbox, click the **Selection** tool.

Selection

4. Click the text object to select it.

5. On the **Object** menu, click **Convert Object to Path**.

Expression Design converts the text object into a group of vector paths.

> **Tip** The paths in a converted text object are grouped by default, meaning that Expression Design treats them as one object. To break apart the group and treat the characters of the text as separate objects, click Ungroup on the Arrange menu.

Zoom

Lasso Selection

6. In the Toolbox, click the **Zoom** tool.

7. Drag a selection marquee around the letter **i** in **smile**, and release the mouse button to zoom in on this letter.

8. In the Toolbox, click the **Lasso Selection** tool. (Look for this tool in the **Direct Selection** tool's group.)

9. Drag a selection marquee around the dot of the **i**.

Expression Design selects the dot.

> **Tip** You might wonder why you need the Lasso Selection tool for this particular step. The reason is that Expression Design treats the dot of the *i* as part of the *i*'s path, even though the two elements don't physically touch. Selecting the dot with the Direct Selection tool or the Group Selection tool also selects the rest of the character, which doesn't help you when you want to remove only the dot.

10. Press ⌽Del⌿, or click **Delete** on the **Edit** menu.

Expression Design deletes the dot, which would not be possible if you hadn't converted the text object into a group of paths.

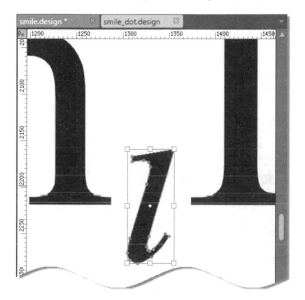

11. In the Toolbox, click the **Selection** tool.

12. Switch to the *smile_dot.design* document by clicking its flip tab in the flip bar.

13. Select the replacement dot by clicking it.

14. On the **Edit** menu, click **Copy**.

Expression Design copies the replacement dot to the Clipboard.

15. Switch back to *smile.design* by clicking its flip tab in the flip bar.

16. On the **Edit** menu, click **Paste**.

Expression Design pastes the replacement dot into the Text layer.

17. With the **Selection** tool, drag the replacement dot to the desired position in the layout.

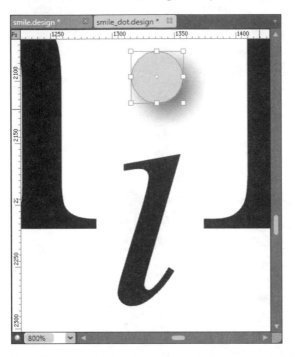

Your finished design is now ready to save or print.

CLOSE the *smile.design* and *smile_dot.design* files without saving any changes. If you are not continuing directly to the next chapter, exit Expression Design.

Key Points

- A text object is a special kind of vector graphic that contains typographical characters or glyphs. Glyphs remain editable as text, not as graphics.

- You use the Text tool to create text objects and edit their glyphs.

- From the Properties panel, you can set many different style attributes for text objects, including general appearance attributes such as fill and stroke colors as well as text-only attributes such as typeface and leading. Most attributes can apply to individual glyphs as well as the entire text object, but some apply only to the entire text object.

- With Expression Design, you can attach text to a path, by which you effectively use the contour of the path as the baseline of the text.

- With Expression Design, you can also create area text, in which you use the interior of a path as the container for the text.

- At times, you might need a greater level of control over the structure or appearance of your text than text objects by themselves give you. Therefore, with Expression Design, you can convert any text object into an identical group of standard vector paths. These paths look and read exactly like glyphs, but do not retain their editability as text. You edit them with the vector tools instead.

Chapter at a Glance

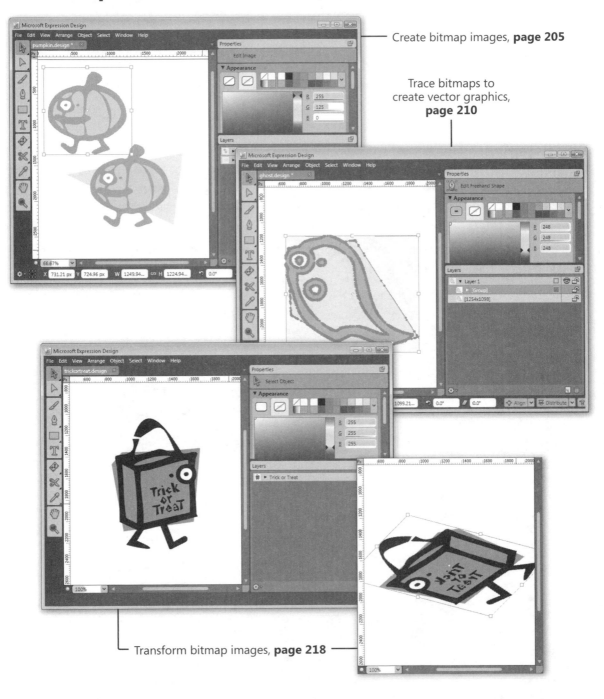

Create bitmap images, **page 205**

Trace bitmaps to create vector graphics, **page 210**

Transform bitmap images, **page 218**

9 Working with Bitmap Images

In this chapter, you will learn to:

✔ Import artwork in vector and bitmap formats.

✔ Create bitmap images.

✔ Trace bitmaps to create vector graphics.

✔ Transform bitmap images.

Microsoft Expression Design is primarily a tool for creating and editing vector graphics, yet its relationship with the world of vectors is not entirely an exclusive one. If you so desire—and many do—you can include bitmap (raster) images in your designs.

As you will recall from Chapter 1, "Working with Documents," bitmaps are pixel based. They don't contain anchor points or segments, and they don't have strokes, fills, or other appearance attributes. These raster images are simply grids of colored squares. As such, you cannot change their content or structure by using Expression Design's vector-editing tools. You can, however, place bitmaps in your document window and transform them with the Selection tool. You can create a new bitmap image from existing vector objects through a process called rasterization, and you can create a new vector group from a bitmap graphic through a process called *auto tracing*.

In this chapter, you will explore these and other features.

> **Important** Before you can use the practice files in this chapter, you need to install them from the book's companion CD to their default location. See "Using the Book's CD" at the beginning of this book for more information.

> **Troubleshooting** Graphics and operating system–related instructions in this book reflect the Windows Vista user interface. If your computer is running Windows XP and you experience trouble following the instructions as written, please refer to the "Information for Readers Running Windows XP" section at the beginning of this book.

Importing Artwork in Vector and Bitmap (Raster) Formats

There are three main ways to bring existing artwork into Expression Design, as follows:

- **Opening.** To open existing artwork, click Open on the File menu. In the Open File dialog box, navigate to the file you want, and double-click the file's icon. Expression Design opens a brand new document window for the file.

  You know from Chapter 1 that you can open documents in the following formats: Expression Design, Photoshop (.psd), .tiff, .jpeg, .gif, .png, .bmp, Windows Media Photo (.wmp), and ICO. Of these, only Expression Design documents are in a native vector format. The rest open as pixel-based graphics or *image objects*.

  When you open a file that isn't in Expression Design format, the artwork displays as a single image object on a single layer. (If the original artwork consists of multiple layers, Expression Design flattens them to a single layer.) The default dimensions of the artboard match the dimensions of the image object exactly. As you'll recall from Chapter 1, the artboard is the frame inside the document window that represents the document's imageable area. Objects inside the artboard are printable and exportable; objects outside the artboard are not.

  > **Tip** You can change the artboard's dimensions by clicking Artboard Size on the File menu.

- **Importing.** To import existing artwork, open any Expression Design file or create a new file, then click Import in the File menu. The Import File dialog box opens. Navigate to the desired file using the controls in the dialog box, and double-click the file's icon. Expression Design places the file on the currently selected layer of the current document window. The size of the artboard does not change when you import a file.

  Expression Design lets you import all the openable file formats except, ironically, .design files. You can, however, freely copy the contents of .design files and paste them into other Expression Design documents—more on that in a moment.

  In addition, you can import Adobe Acrobat (.pdf) files created in Adobe Illustrator as well as the original Adobe Illustrator (.ai) files, provided that they were saved with the Create PDF Compatible File option enabled. You cannot import other kinds of Acrobat or Illustrator files.

- **Pasting.** To paste existing artwork, first select the artwork, then copy or cut it. You can copy artwork created in a different program or in an Expression Design document. Switch to the destination document window in Expression Design, and select the desired layer in the Layers panel. Then open the Edit menu and click one of the following commands:

  - **Paste.** Click Paste to insert the contents of the Clipboard in the middle of the current view of the document window at the top of the current layer's stacking order.

  - **Paste in Front.** Click Paste In Front to insert the contents of the Clipboard in the same position on the screen as the copied objects were (if applicable). This command places them at the top of the current layer's stacking order. If you select an existing object before you paste, Expression Design inserts the contents of the Clipboard one step above this object in the stacking order.

    > **Tip** Even though image objects are not vector graphics, you can stack them on a layer. You can even mix them with other kinds of objects on the same layer.

  - **Paste in Back.** Click Paste In Back to insert the contents of the Clipboard at the same position on the screen as the copied objects were (again, if applicable). This command places them at the bottom of the current layer's stacking order. Select an existing object first if you want to insert the contents of the Clipboard one step below it in the stacking order.

  - **Paste with Layer.** When you paste with the other pasting commands, Expression Design automatically places all copied objects on a single layer, even if you cut or copied them from multiple layers. Click Paste With Layer to maintain the original layer assignments of the cut or copied objects. If the destination document does not have corresponding layers, Expression Design creates new layers to match the ones on the Clipboard.

    > **Tip** When you use the Paste with Layer command, Expression Design ignores the currently selected layer in the Layers panel. The layer selection does not determine the location of the pasted artwork.

  - **Paste Special.** Click Paste Special to change the format of the contents of the Clipboard. When you invoke this command, the Paste Format dialog box opens, showing all available formats based on the type of data on the Clipboard.

(Depending on what you have copied, you might only receive a single format option.) Select the desired format, and then click OK. The Paste Special dialog box closes, and Expression Design pastes the contents of the Clipboard to the current layer at the top of the stacking order in the specified format.

> **Tip** Unfortunately, the current version of Expression Design does not support some of the most common vector formats, including Encapsulated PostScript (.eps), Windows Metafile (.wmf), and Flash (.swf). You cannot open, import, or paste these formats as vector graphics; however, in some cases, Expression Design creates image objects of the vectors if you copy them in their native application and then place them in your document window using the Paste command.

Therefore, with regard to image objects in particular, your choice to open, import, or paste depends on the needs of your project, as follows:

- Open an image object to display it in its own document window on a custom-sized artboard.

- Import an image object to bring it into the selected layer of the current document window.

- Paste an image object that you have copied from another document window or application, or paste a vector graphic copied from another application as a bitmap with the Paste Special command.

In this exercise, you will add bitmap images to an Expression Design document using the Import command and the Paste command.

> **USE** the *berries.bmp* and *leaves.bmp* files. These practice files are located in the *Documents\Microsoft Press\Expression Design SBS\WorkingBitmap* folder.
> **BE SURE TO** start Expression Design before beginning this exercise.

1. On the **File** menu, click **New**.

   The New Document dialog box opens.

2. In the **Name** field, type **Photos**.

3. On the **Presets** menu, click **Letter**.

4. Set the resolution to **300 px/inch**.

   The resolution of the digital photo that you will import is 300 pixels per inch. Setting the resolution of the document window to the same resolution as the imported image ensures that Expression Design does not process the pixels of the image object, which preserves the image quality.

> **Tip** If the resolution of the document window does not match the resolution of the image object, Expression Design processes the pixels of the image to match the resolution of the document window, which adversely affects image quality. When the resolutions are too far apart, the loss of image quality can be quite noticeable.

5. Click **OK**.

The New Document dialog box closes, and Expression Design opens the new document window to your specifications.

6. On the **File** menu, click **Import**.

The Import Document dialog box opens.

7. In the **Import Document** dialog box, navigate to *berries.bmp*, and double-click it.

The Import Document dialog box closes, and Expression Design imports the bitmap as an image object to the current layer.

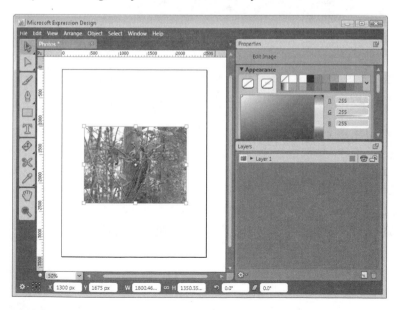

Now try opening a bitmap directly.

8. On the **File** menu, click **Open**.

   The Open File dialog box opens.

9. Navigate to the *leaves.bmp* file, and double-click it.

   Expression Design opens the bitmap in its own document window.

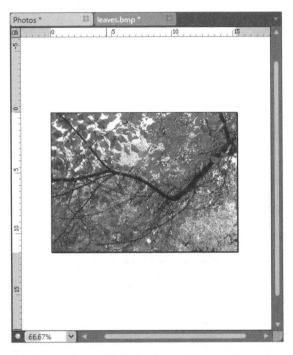

Selection

10. In the Toolbox, click the **Selection** tool.

11. Click the digital photo in the *leaves.bmp* document window to select it.

12. On the **Edit** menu, click **Copy** to copy the bitmap to the Clipboard.

13. Switch to the document window that contains the digital photo with the berries by clicking its flip tab in the flip bar.

14. On the **Edit** menu, click **Paste**.

    Expression Design pastes the contents of the Clipboard as a new image object. Depending on your view of the document window, the pasted photo might completely superimpose the photo with the berries.

15. With the **Selection** tool, arrange the photos in the document window so that both are visible.

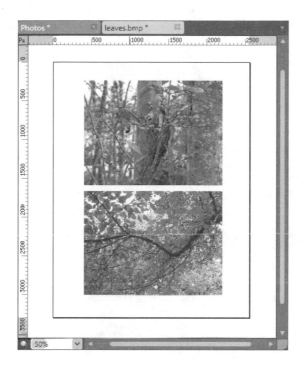

> **Tip** Image objects behave just like other objects in Expression Design. You can move them around in the document window by dragging them with the Selection tool and, as you will learn later in this chapter, you can apply transformations to them.

Your finished document is now ready to save or print.

CLOSE all open documents without saving any changes.

Creating Bitmap Images

Expression Design includes a handy feature that lets you create a bitmap image from any rectangular region in the document window. This process is somewhat like taking a photo. Whatever is visible inside the specified region is included in the new image object, while the original objects—the vectors, text objects, or bitmaps that you captured—remain unchanged.

In this exercise, you will create a bitmap object from an existing vector graphic.

> **USE** the *pumpkin.design* file. This practice file is located in the *Documents\Microsoft Press\ Expression Design SBS\WorkingBitmap* folder.
>
> **OPEN** the *pumpkin.design* file.

1. Note that the illustration contains two layers: one with a vector image of a cartoon pumpkin, and one with a vector background element.

The background layer is locked to keep you from accidentally selecting its object.

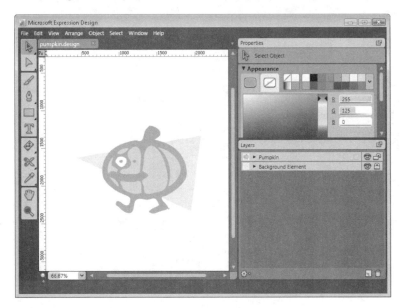

2. On the **File** menu, click **Document Size**.

The Document Size dialog box opens.

3. Make a mental note that the resolution of the document window is 300 pixels per inch, and click **OK**.

The Document Size dialog box closes.

4. In the **Layers** panel, click the **Toggle Layer Visibility** button (the eye) of the **Background Element** layer.

Visibility On

Expression Design renders the background element invisible. Now you can create an image object from the pumpkin illustration by itself.

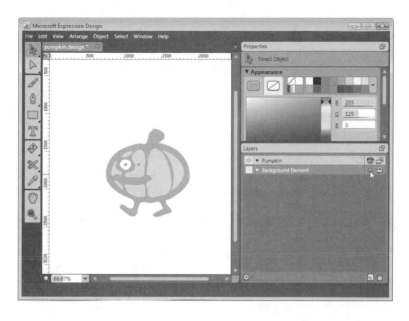

> **Tip** If you do not hide the background element, Expression Design will include it in the image object.

5. In the **Layers** panel, click the **Pumpkin** layer to select it.

6. On the **Object** menu, point to **Image**, and then click **Create Image Object**.

Create
Image Object

The pointer changes into crosshairs with a bitmap picture.

7. Point to the upper-left corner of the region that you want to capture.

Choose a position close to the upper bounds of the pumpkin illustration.

8. Hold down the mouse button, and drag toward the lower-right corner of the region that you want to capture.

Expression Design draws a marquee around the selected region.

9. Release the mouse button.

The Rasterize Area dialog box opens.

10. Set the resolution to **300 px/inch**.

When the resolution of the image object matches the resolution of the document window, Expression Design does not have to process the pixels of the image object, which preserves the image quality. You determined already that the resolution of the document window is 300 pixels per inch, so your specified resolution is a perfect match.

> **Tip** Just as when you are importing an image object, your specified resolution does not have to match the resolution of the document window, but in the event that it does not, Expression Design will process the pixels of the image object to get it to fit. Depending on the disparity between the two resolutions, you might notice some loss of image quality.

11. Click **OK**.

The Rasterize Area dialog box closes, and Expression Design creates the image object from the visible portion of the selection marquee. The new bitmap appears directly on top of the original vector illustration.

> **Tip** All visible elements in the selection marquee become part of the image object. It doesn't matter if these elements are vector objects, bitmap objects, or text objects, and it doesn't matter if they appear on different layers. If you hadn't hidden the background element at the beginning of this exercise, Expression Design would have included it in the image object.

Selection

12. In the Toolbox, click the **Selection** tool.

13. In the **Layers** panel, click the **Toggle Layer Visibility** button to display the **Background Element** layer.

Visibility Off

The background element is shown again behind the vector version of the pumpkin illustration.

14. Drag the new image object to a different location in the document window so that the bitmap and vector versions are both visible at the same time.

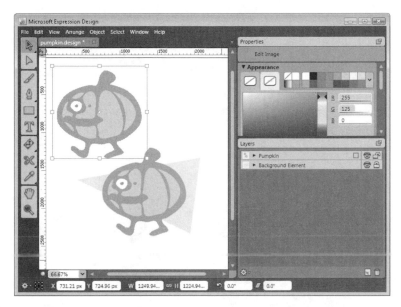

Zoom

15. In the Toolbox, click the **Zoom** tool.

16. Drag a marquee around one of the eyes in the vector version of the pumpkin.

Expression Design zooms in close to the eye. Notice that the vector version retains its sharpness at very high magnification levels.

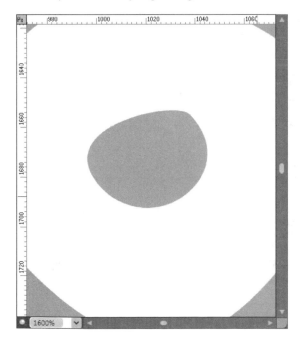

17. On the **View** menu, click **Fit to Screen**.

Expression Design zooms back out so that both objects are visible.

18. With the **Zoom** tool, drag a marquee around one of the eyes in the bitmap version of the pumpkin.

Expression Design zooms in close again; the boxy shape of the pixels in the bitmap version is clearly visible.

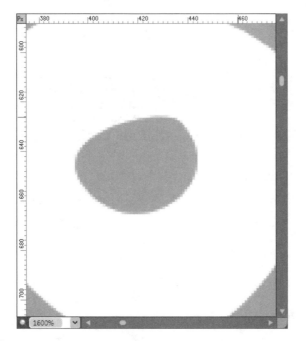

19. On the **View** menu, click **Fit to Screen**.

Expression Design zooms back out. Your image is ready to save or print.

CLOSE the *pumpkin.design* file without saving any changes.

Tracing Bitmaps to Create Vector Graphics

In the previous section, you transformed a vector image into a bitmap object. You might be wondering if it is possible to do the reverse: take a bitmap image and turn it into a vector graphic.

The answer is a qualified yes. Expression Design's Auto Trace feature examines the pixels in a bitmap graphic, looks for shapes and patterns, and automatically draws vector paths on top of them—which is why it's referred to as *tracing*.

Traced bitmaps are path based, not pixel based, and they come with all the advantages of vector graphics. They are resolution independent, so you can transform them as much as you wish without affecting image quality.

Unfortunately, tracing is not an exact science, and raster graphics and vector graphics are so different that, more often than not, you lose a great deal of detail in the translation process, as the following image shows. Traced bitmaps also tend to be structurally unwieldy. Even though you are free to modify them with all the vector-editing tools at your disposal, the paths contain so many anchor points and segments that they are almost impossible to edit in any kind of useful way.

Tip If you are an experienced vector artist, you can always trace a bitmap graphic the old-fashioned way: Place the bitmap on a layer of its own, and lock this layer in the Layers panel. Then create a new layer directly on top of it, and manually trace the bitmap using the Paintbrush and Pen tools.

Finally, there is so much visual information in a typical bitmap graphic that a similar-looking vector translation is very hard to achieve, particularly when you attempt to trace a digital photo. Tracing works best with very simple bitmaps—ones that already have that flat, clean vector look. If your goal is to create a decent-looking vector photo with all its subtle shifts in tone and hue, you are bound to be disappointed by today's technology.

In this exercise, you will use Expression Design's Auto Trace feature to make a vector version of a bitmap graphic.

USE the *ghost.design* file. This practice file is located in the *Documents\Microsoft Press\Expression Design SBS\WorkingBitmap* folder.

OPEN the *ghost.design* practice file.

1. Take a look at the file. It contains an imported bitmap image of a cartoon ghost.

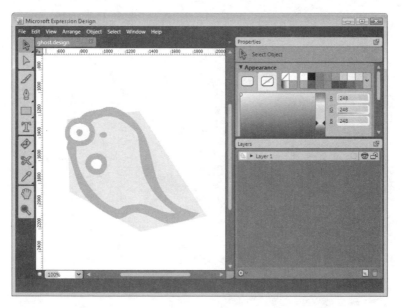

2. In the **Layers** panel, expand the contents of the **Layer1** layer.

   There is a single object: the ghost bitmap itself, indicated by its dimensions of 1254 by 1098 pixels. Keep the layer contents expanded; you'll come back to this panel in a later step.

Selection

3. In the Toolbox, click the **Selection** tool.

4. Select the bitmap image by clicking it.

5. On the **Object** menu, point to **Image**, and then click **Auto Trace Image**.

The Auto Trace Image dialog box opens.

6. In the **Number of colors** field, type **5**.

This option determines the total number of colors in the vector image. You can choose a preset value from the menu or type a custom value directly into the field.

> **Tip** More isn't always better when it comes to colors, particularly if you are tracing a photograph. Almost all digital photos contain subtle shifts in tone and hue, resulting in massive amounts of visual information. You might be tempted to specify a high number of colors in your traced vector image to make it seem more realistic, but the result tends to be artificial-looking banding, along with way too many vector objects to manage. The simple truth of the matter is that vectors just aren't that good at conveying photorealistic images.

7. On the **Pre-filtering** menu, click **4**.

This option determines the degree to which Expression Design applies smoothing to the bitmap before tracing it. The higher the value, the more pronounced the effect. The None setting maximizes sharpness, but since pixels are rectangular in shape, you might introduce some unwanted jaggedness into your vector paths if you use this setting.

8. On the **Tightness of fit** menu, click **Medium**.

This option determines how closely Expression Design traces the bitmap. The tighter the fit, the more detail you capture but the greater the complexity of the paths, which makes the traced image harder to edit and manage.

Auto Trace Image		
Number of colors	5 ▾	OK
Pre-filtering	4 ▾	Cancel
Tightness of fit	Medium ▾	

9. Click **OK**.

Expression Design traces the bitmap and places the result as a group of vector objects directly on top of the bitmap in the same layer.

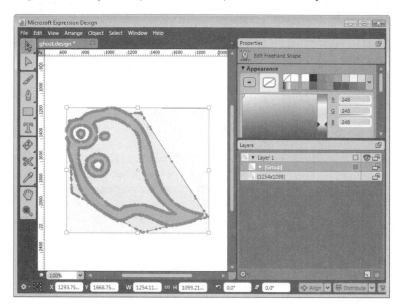

> **Tip** Unless you have a lot of experience tracing bitmaps, you won't find it easy to predict what the results of the various parameters will be. For this reason, you might try running the Auto Trace command several times under different settings. This way, you can compare the results side by side. Keep the vector group that looks the best, and delete the others.

Now that you have a path-based ghost, you can edit it using all the vector-editing tools and commands at your disposal.

10. In the **Layers** panel, click to select the original bitmap ghost.

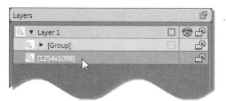

Expression Design selects this object in the document window.

11. Press the [Del] key, or click **Delete** on the **Edit** menu.

Expression Design deletes the original bitmap image, leaving you with the vector group.

In your vector version of the ghost, notice the pale gray paths that represent the white background of the bitmap image. You don't need them, so get rid of them.

Direct Selection

12. In the Toolbox, click the **Direct Selection** tool.

The vector objects are in a group, so the Direct Selection tool lets you select the individual paths within the group.

> **Tip** To ungroup the vector objects so that you can manipulate them individually, select the group, and then click Ungroup on the Arrange menu.

13. Hold down the [Shift] key and click the pale gray paths.

Expression Design selects the paths.

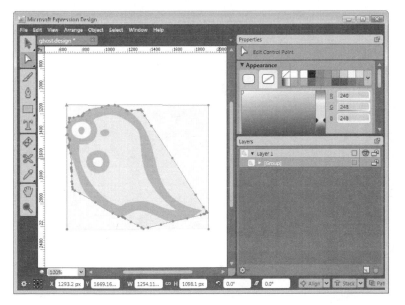

14. Press [Del], or click **Delete** on the **Edit** menu.

Expression Design deletes these unneeded paths.

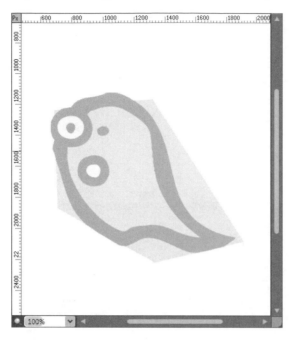

Now try a different kind of edit.

15. With the **Direct Selection** tool, click the light blue interior of the vector ghost.

Expression Design selects the corresponding path.

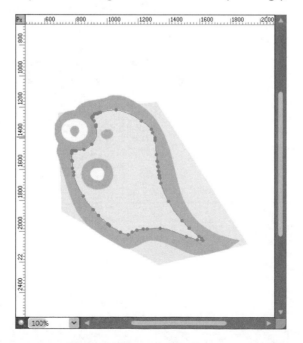

16. In the **Properties** panel, in the **Appearance** category, set the fill of this path to white (R255, G255, B255).

Expression Design instantly changes the color of the ghost.

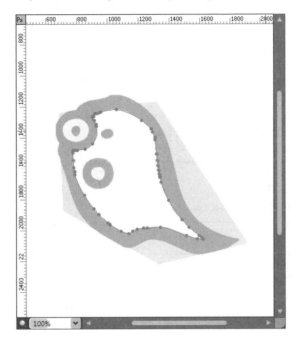

> **Tip** Feel free to experiment with other kinds of edits and transformations to the vector group.

Your design is now ready to save or print.

 CLOSE the *ghost.design* file without saving any changes.

Transforming Bitmap Images

When you select a bitmap object with the Selection tool, a bounding box with square handles is displayed around it, indicating that the object can be transformed. In Expression Design, you can do the following:

Rotate Pointer

- **Rotate the bitmap.** To rotate a selected bitmap manually with the Selection tool, activate that tool and point to any of the corner handles. When the pointer changes to a curved two-way arrow, drag in the direction you want to rotate the bitmap.

> **Tip** You can constrain the angle of rotation to increments of 45 degrees by holding down the Shift key while rotating the bitmap.

To rotate the bitmap by a precise amount, you can use the Action Bar. Type a value (in degrees) in the Rotation Angle slider, and press Enter.

> **Tip** Changing the position of the bitmap's center point affects how Expression Design applies a transformation, and this is particularly true with rotations. Think of the center point as a thumbtack around which the bitmap rotates. To move the center point, you can simply drag it to another location in the document window; you can even move it off the surface of the bitmap! For quick adjustments to the center point's position, you can use the Action Bar. When you click one of the white squares on the Registration Point button, Expression Design moves the center point to the corresponding preset location on the object's bounding box.

Another way to rotate the bitmap is to point to Transform on the Arrange menu and then click Rotate 90° Clockwise, Rotate 90° Counter Clockwise, or Rotate 180°.

Skew Pointer

- **Skew the bitmap.** Skewing tilts the object along one of its axes. To skew a selected bitmap manually with the Selection tool, point to any of the side handles. When the pointer changes to the skew symbol, drag in the direction you want to skew the bitmap.

> **Tip** Hold down Alt to skew the bitmap around its center point.

To skew the bitmap by a precise amount, you can type a value (in degrees) in the Skew Angle field in the Action Bar and press Enter.

Scale Pointer

- **Scale, stretch, or compress the bitmap.** To scale, stretch, or compress a selected bitmap manually with the Selection tool, position the mouse pointer on any of the handles. When the pointer changes to a straight two-way arrow, drag in the direction you want to alter the bitmap.

> **Tip** Hold down Shift as you drag to maintain the original proportions of the bitmap.

To scale, stretch, or compress the bitmap by a precise amount, you can type values in the Width or Height field in the Action Bar and press Enter. Click the link picture between the two fields to toggle the constraint on the bitmap's proportions.

- **Reflect the bitmap.** To reflect (flip) a selected bitmap, point to Transform on the Arrange menu, and click Reflect Horizontal or Reflect Vertical.

> **Tip** To undo all transformations, point to Transform on the Arrange menu, and then click Reset Transform. To set all transformations as permanent, click Reset Bounding Box on the Transform submenu. (Even if you reset the bounding box, the bitmap image is still editable; you just can't undo the transformations with the Reset Transform command.)

Because vector graphics and text objects are path based, they can be transformed without any loss in image quality whatsoever. However, bitmap objects are pixel based, and they do not come with the same guarantee. In fact, almost *any* transformation affects bitmap image quality for the worse, especially with regard to scaling. Smaller transformations are less egregious than bigger ones, though, so when you transform a bitmap object, be very careful that you don't overdo it.

> **Tip** Scaling down (decreasing the dimensions) is generally much kinder to bitmaps than scaling up. When you scale down, Expression Design gets rid of a certain number of pixels in the image, but the dimensions of the object are smaller, so you tend not to notice. When you scale up, Expression Design actually adds pixels to the image by duplicating those that already exist. You end up magnifying the rectangular shape of the pixels, and as a result, your image starts to exhibit a certain blockiness or lack of sharpness.

In this exercise, you will transform a bitmap graphic three times using three different methods: rotating manually with the Selection tool, using the Action Bar to skew by a precise amount, and using a menu command to reflect the image. Then you will undo all the transformations with the Reset Transform command.

> **USE** the *trickortreat.design* file. This practice file is located in the *Documents\Microsoft Press\Expression Design SBS\WorkingBitmap* folder.
>
> **OPEN** the *trickortreat.design* file.

1. Examine the file.

   It contains an imported bitmap image of a walking trick-or-treat bag.

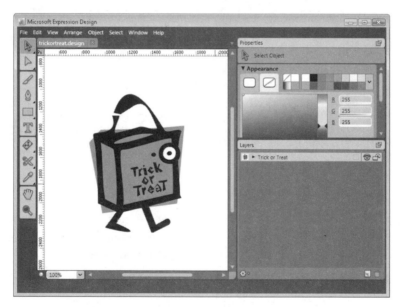

2. In the Toolbox, click the **Selection** tool.

Selection

3. Click the bitmap object to select it.

   Expression Design shows the bitmap's bounding box.

4. Point to one of the corner handles.

   The mouse pointer changes to a curved two-way arrow.

Rotate Pointer

5. Drag in the direction you want to rotate the object.

   Expression Design rotates the bitmap object.

6. Go to the Action Bar and set the **Skew Angle** field to **30°**.

Expression Design skews the bitmap object by this amount.

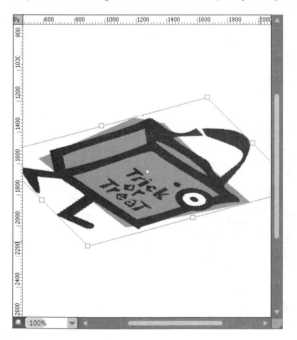

7. On the **Arrange** menu, point to **Transform**, and then click **Reflect Horizontal**.

Expression Design reflects the bitmap object on its horizontal axis. Notice that the text on the graphic is now reversed (a mirror image).

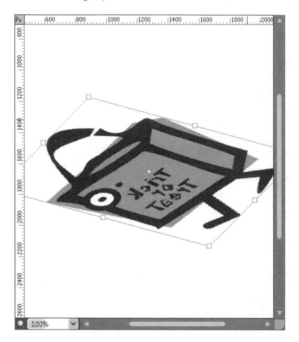

8. On the **Arrange** menu, point to **Transform**, and then click **Reset Transform**.

Expression Design discards all three transformations, and the bitmap image displays as it did in its original state.

CLOSE the *trickortreat.design* file without saving any changes. If you are not continuing directly on to the next chapter, exit Expression Design.

Key Points

- When you open a file, Expression Design places it in its own document window on a custom-fitted artboard.

- When you import a file, Expression Design places it in the selected layer of the current document window. You can import specific kinds of PDF and Adobe Illustrator files in addition to all the openable formats, with the exception of Expression Design files.

- You can paste an image copied from another application with the Paste Special command, which lets you change the format of the image.

- Expression Design lets you create a new bitmap image from any rectangular area in the document window. All visible elements in the selected region are included in this new image object.

- Expression Design's Auto Trace feature detects patterns and shapes in a bitmap and creates matching vector graphics. The result is a vector version of the bitmap. However, because most bitmaps contain more visual information than is suitable or practical for vector graphics, your level of success with Auto Trace will vary.

- Image objects, just like vector graphics and text objects, can be transformed in a wide variety of ways. However, because image objects are pixel-based, most transformations reduce image quality to some degree.

Chapter at a Glance

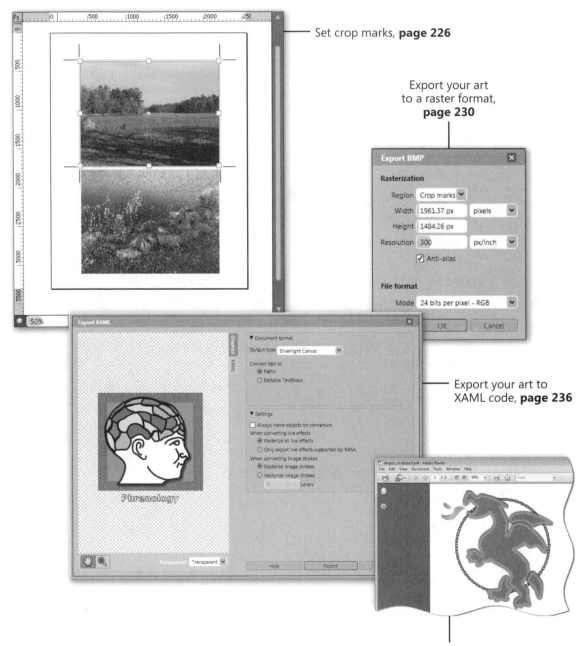

Set crop marks, **page 226**

Export your art to a raster format, **page 230**

Export your art to XAML code, **page 236**

Export your art to PDF, **page 242**

10 Exporting and Printing Your Work

In this chapter, you will learn to:

✔ Set crop marks.

✔ Export your art to a raster format.

✔ Export image objects from the document window.

✔ Export your art to XAML code.

✔ Export your art to PDF.

✔ Print your art.

A graphic designer doesn't work (or play) in a vacuum. Clients and employers require results; your developer colleagues want your finished concept so that they can get busy programming it; and your friends and family count on you for a steady stream of visual entertainment. All are expecting delivery. How do you deliver from Microsoft Expression Design?

In this chapter, you will learn how to export files and make prints.

 Important Before you can use the practice files in this chapter, you need to install them from the book's companion CD to their default location. See "Using the Book's CD" at the beginning of this book for more information.

Troubleshooting Graphics and operating system–related instructions in this book reflect the Windows Vista user interface. If your computer is running Windows XP and you experience trouble following the instructions as written, please refer to the "Information for Readers Running Windows XP" section at the beginning of this book.

Setting Crop Marks

Normally in Expression Design, all visible elements that are within the artboard of the document window are included when you export or print the file—including any white space between the objects themselves and the artboard's frame. To reduce the size of the margins, or to restrict the output to a particular region on the artboard, you can set crop marks. Everything inside the crop marks is exported or printed; everything outside them is ignored.

> **Tip** Hidden elements or elements that are outside the frame of the artboard are always excluded from exporting and printing.

You can set crop marks in three ways:

- **Setting the crop marks manually.** For this method, you drag the mouse to set a rectangular crop region. This way is good and fast, and the visually-oriented graphic designer within you approves, but it isn't as mathematically precise as the other methods.

  To set crop marks manually, point to Crop Marks on the File menu, and click Set. Then drag the mouse over the desired region in the document window.

- **Entering precise values for the crop marks.** For this method, you define the crop region in terms of its x-y coordinates. This method makes great sense to a computer, but it isn't so convenient for a human. Positioning the crop marks with x-y coordinates rarely yields satisfactory results on the first attempt. If you go this route, be prepared for trial and error.

> **Tip** Before you set the crop marks, you could use the values in the X and Y fields in the Action Bar to help you determine the correct coordinates.

  To enter precise values for the crop marks, point to Crop Marks on the File menu, and click Set. Then click anywhere in the document window. When the Set Crop Marks dialog box opens, type values for the upper-left coordinate and the lower-right coordinate of the crop region, and click OK.

- **Setting the crop marks from an object's bounding box.** For this method, you select an object in the document window and use its bounding box as the crop region. This way, the crop marks fit the object precisely, although you can add some white space between the crop marks and the selected object if you so choose.

  To set the crop marks from an object's bounding box, click the object with the Selection tool. Then, on the File menu, point to Crop Marks, and click From Bounding Box.

In this exercise, you will set crop marks first by setting them manually and then by deriving them from the bounding box of an object.

USE the *water.design* file. This practice file is located in the *Documents\Microsoft Press\ Expression Design SBS\ExportingWork* folder.

BE SURE TO start Expression Design before beginning this exercise.

OPEN the *water.design* file.

1. Look at the document. It contains one layer with two image objects, both of them digital photos of the same body of water, arranged one above the other.

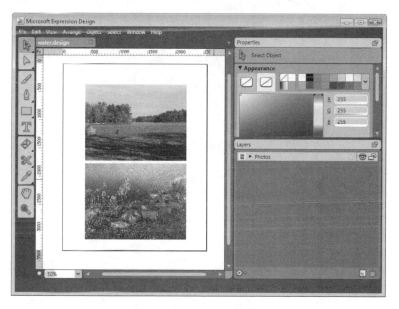

First you will draw the crop marks manually, and then you will reset the crop marks to the bounding box of one of the photos.

2. On the **File** menu, point to **Crop Marks**, and then click **Set**.

    The pointer changes to a crosshair symbol, and horizontal and vertical positioning rules extend from it across the entire document window.

3. Point to the upper-left corner of the top photo in the empty part of the document window. Then drag down to the lower-right corner of the bottom photo.

    Tip The crop region consists of the entire area of the rectangle that you draw, including whatever margins or white space you leave around the objects themselves.

Expression Design adds crop marks to the document window to match the dimensions of the specified region. If you were to print or export this document now, you would get only whatever is inside the crop marks; Expression Design would ignore the extra white space outside the crop marks.

Tip If the white space inside your crop marks is a little off-balance—too much at the top, for example, or too little along the sides—you can redraw the crop marks by repeating steps 2 and 3, or you can simply reposition the objects inside the crop marks by dragging them with the Selection tool.

---

4. On the **File** menu, point to **Crop Marks**, and then click **Remove**.

Expression Design removes the crop marks that you just placed.

Selection

5. In the Toolbox, click the **Selection** tool. Then click the upper photo to select it.

6. On the **File** menu, point to **Crop Marks**, and then click **From Bounding Box**.

The Set Crop Marks dialog box opens.

7. In the **Extra border width** field, type **12 px**.

Extra white space appears around the photo.

> **Tip** If you prefer to set the crop marks exactly on the edge of the object's bounding box, type *0 px* in the Extra Border Width field.

8. Click **OK**.

Expression Design sets the crop marks around the upper photo's bounding box. Now when you print or export this document, you get only the top photo (with 12-pixel margins on all four sides).

Your finished document is now ready to save or print. If you opt to save, Expression Design includes the crop marks just as you positioned them but does not delete the objects outside the crop marks.

CLOSE the *water.design* file without saving any changes.

Exporting Your Art to a Raster Format

Expression Design lets you export your artwork to a variety of raster (pixel-based) formats: Photoshop (.psd), .tiff, .jpeg, .bmp, .png, .gif, and Windows Media Photo (.wpd). Not every application can display vector (path-based) art, so exporting your documents as pixel-based images makes it easier for you to share them with your friends and family.

For the purposes of the export, your paths are converted to pixels. However, Expression Design does not permanently rasterize the actual objects on your artboard; anything in vector format retains its vector editability in the original Expression Design document.

> **Tip** To change general export settings, point to Options on the Edit menu, and then click Print And Export.

In this exercise, you will export a vector graphic as a .bmp file.

> **USE** the *keyboard.design* file. This practice file is located in the *Documents\Microsoft Press\ Expression Design SBS\ExportingWork* folder.
>
> **OPEN** the *keyboard.design* file.

1. Take a look at this illustration, which uses a group of vector objects to depict one full octave on a piano keyboard. We have placed crop marks in this document already to save you the trouble of doing it yourself.

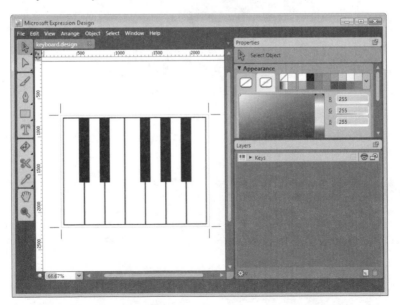

> **Tip** If there aren't any crop marks visible in the document window, Expression Design exports the entire artboard. Anything outside the artboard's frame is excluded in the exported bitmap.

2. On the **File** menu, click **Export**.

The Export dialog box opens.

> **Tip** You can bypass the Export dialog box by selecting the object or objects that you want to export and clicking Copy on the Edit menu. Then switch to another application—Microsoft Office Word, for instance—and paste the contents of the Clipboard into a new document. Using this method, you will get a pixel-based image, even if you copied vector graphics, unless you paste into an application that understands the vector data format that Expression Design uses. (However, if you attempt to export a text object by way of the Clipboard, you might get plain text when you paste it in the target application.)

3. On the **Save as type** menu, click **BMP (*.bmp)**.

By default, Expression Design exports the file in Windows Bitmap format. If you prefer a different format, click the format you want on the Save As Type menu.

You can type a name for the exported file in the File Name field, or do nothing and use the name that Expression Design automatically supplies.

> **Tip** When you export a previously saved file, Expression Design supplies the same file name as the saved version.

4. In the **Export** dialog box, retain the default name, navigate to the folder where you want Expression Design to save the exported file (such as the *Pictures* folder), and then click **Save**.

Expression Design exports the .bmp file to this location.

The Export dialog box closes, and the Export BMP dialog box opens. This dialog box presents options specific for the .bmp format. If you had chosen a different export format in step 3, Expression Design would open a different dialog box here with different options.

> **Tip** For detailed information on each of the dialog boxes for the various export formats, click User Guide on the Help menu.

5. On the **Region** menu, click **Crop marks**.

Under this setting, Expression Design includes only the cropped region in the exported .bmp.

6. Select the **Anti-alias** check box, if it is not already selected.

Anti-aliasing is a common trick to make the edges of pixel-based graphics appear smoother and less blocky. It works on the principle of an optical illusion, by blending the colors of the pixels on the edge of a figure with the colors of the background pixels. For most pieces of art, anti-aliasing makes good sense. Disable this option only when you know for sure that you don't want the smoothing effect.

> **Tip** To ignore the crop marks and export the entire artboard, click Canvas on the Region menu.

7. Click **OK**.

> **Tip** For .bmp files and most other export formats, Expression Design lets you specify the dimensions and resolution of the exported file by changing the values in the Width, Height, and Resolution fields. You cannot change the dimensions of the exported file when you choose PDF as the export format.

The Export BMP dialog box closes, and Expression Design exports the design in .bmp format. Here, we'll prove it to you.

8. On the **File** menu, click **Open**. Then navigate to the location of the exported .bmp, and double-click the file's icon.

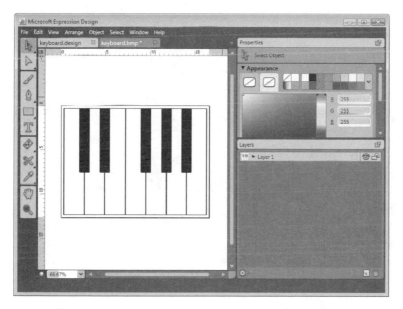

Expression Design opens the .bmp version of the keyboard in its own document window.

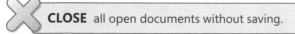
CLOSE all open documents without saving.

Exporting Image Objects from the Document Window

With Expression Design, you can also export an image object directly from the document window. Using this method, you can create quick raster files in .tiff, .bmp, .png, .jpeg, .gif, or Windows Media Photo (.wdp) format. During the export, you don't get as many options to tweak, but you don't have to fuss with crop marks, either, which might save you some time.

In this exercise, you will export an image object directly from the document window.

> **USE** the *lamp_squirrel.design* file. This practice file is located in the *Documents\Microsoft Press\Expression Design SBS\ExportingWork* folder.
>
> **OPEN** the *lamp_squirrel.design* file.

1. Examine this document, which contains two digital photos—one of a park lamp, and one of a squirrel—without crop marks. You will export the squirrel photo as a separate image file directly from the document window.

Selection

2. In the Toolbox, click the **Selection** tool, and then click the squirrel photo.

    Expression Design selects this image object.

3. On the **Object** menu, point to **Image**, and then click **Export as Image File**.

    The Export Image To File dialog box opens.

4. On the **Save as type** menu, click **Windows Media Photo**.

    Expression Design exports the squirrel photo in WDP format. Again, if you prefer a different format, simply choose a different one from this menu.

5. In the **File name** field, type **squirrel**.

    In this case, you will not use the generic file name that Expression Design supplies, because it is not descriptive enough.

6. Navigate to the *Pictures* folder or some other convenient location on your computer, using the standard controls along the top and down the left side of this dialog box, and then click **Save**.

The Export Image To File dialog box closes, and the Export Windows Media Photo dialog box opens. This dialog box presents options specific for the .wdp format. Different export formats give you different options.

> **Tip** Click User Guide on the Help menu for detailed information on all the different export formats and options. Please note that you cannot change the dimensions or the resolution of the exported image for any of the supported formats when you export the image object directly.

7. Select the **Lossless** check box.

This option refers to the method of file *compression*, which determines the degree to which the information in the image is packed into a smaller and more manageable file.

There are two main types of compression: lossless and lossy. *Lossless* compression makes the resulting image file smaller by organizing the visual information more efficiently. *Lossy* compression organizes the information more efficiently and also throws out a certain amount of extraneous data. Normally the lost information is never missed, because the human eye is easy to trick. But if lossy compression becomes too high, too much information is thrown out, and image quality noticeably degrades.

A lossless .wdp file, then, retains all its original information, so the exported image will look exactly as it does in the document window. (Notice that the Quality slider becomes inactive when you check the Lossless option, a hint that the highest possible quality will be used.) Were you to clear the Lossless check box, the slider determines the level of compression. Reducing quality increases compression, which makes the image file smaller but less visually appealing.

> **Tip** When you reduce the quality in WDP and JPEG files, the exported photo takes up less storage space on your computer, but the image quality degrades—perhaps noticeably so, especially at low quality levels. Each image object is different, so experiment with several different quality settings to find the one that best balances file size and appearance.

8. Click **OK** to close the Export Windows Media Photo dialog box.

Expression Design exports the squirrel photo as a .wdp file.

9. On the **File** menu, click **Open**. Then navigate to the location of the exported .wdp file, and double-click its icon.

Expression Design opens the file in its own document window. As you can tell, you exported the squirrel image only, not the squirrel plus the lamp.

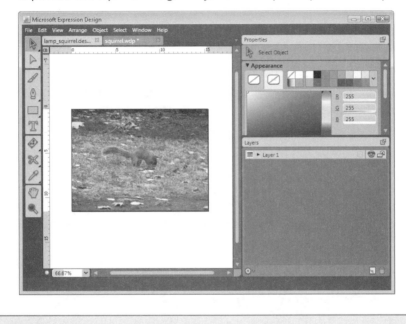

CLOSE all open documents without saving any changes.

Exporting Your Art to XAML Code

Extensible Application Markup Language—*XAML*—is a computer language for describing graphical displays and user interfaces. It translates your layout into plain-text code, which acts very much like step-by-step instructions for drawing the art. An application that understands XAML can "read" these instructions and recreate your layout—no external image files are needed. Newer Windows-based software makes extensive use of XAML behind the scenes, and applications such as Microsoft Expression Blend and the development tools for Microsoft Silverlight can render XAML code in graphical form.

> **Tip** Microsoft Silverlight is a platform for creating rich media presentations and Web applications. In this regard it's similar to Flash. You can learn more about Silverlight at *www.microsoft.com/silverlight/*.

In this exercise, you will export an Expression Design document as an XAML file.

> **USE** the *phrenology.design* file. This practice file is located in the *Documents\Microsoft Press\Expression Design SBS\ExportingWork* folder.
>
> **OPEN** the *phrenology.design* file.

1. Look at this illustration, which is the user interface for a Silverlight application about the discredited science of phrenology. (Phrenology attempts to predict personality traits and behavior by studying the bumps on a person's head.)

This isn't the prettiest graphic in this book, but its shortcomings in the taste department will help us illustrate the effects of XAML translation.

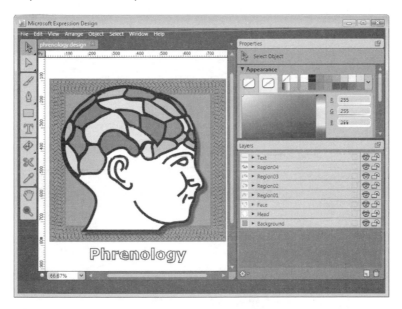

Imagine that, when this application is finished, the user will be able to click the different sections of the human head and receive brief descriptions of their phrenological significance. None of this functionality has been programmed yet; that's all happening later in the Silverlight development environment. The objective here is to get the user interface out of Expression Design in a format that is useful for a Silverlight developer.

This illustration makes use of several Expression Design features. The letters in the word *Phrenology* have a black stroke, there is a drop shadow under the shape of the head, and the background box uses an image stroke.

2. On the **File** menu, click **Export**.

The Export dialog box opens.

3. On the **Save as type** menu, click **XAML (*.xaml)**.

You can type a name for the exported XAML document in the File Name field, or do nothing and use the default name that Expression Design supplies. You gain nothing by changing the default name, unless your naming strategy is to attach suffixes to related files, as in *phrenology_xaml*.

4. For the purposes of this exercise, keep the default name. Navigate to a convenient location on your computer.

Expression Design exports the XAML file to this location. If this really were a Silverlight project, you would probably have a special folder set aside for all project assets. That would be the ideal location for the exported XAML file.

5. Click **Save**.

The Export dialog box closes, and the Export XAML dialog box opens.

> **Tip** You can bypass the Export XAML dialog box by selecting the desired objects and choosing Copy XAML from the Edit menu. Expression Design copies the corresponding XAML code to the Clipboard by using the default format settings and rasterization options. To change these defaults, point to Options on the Edit menu, and then click Clipboard (XAML).

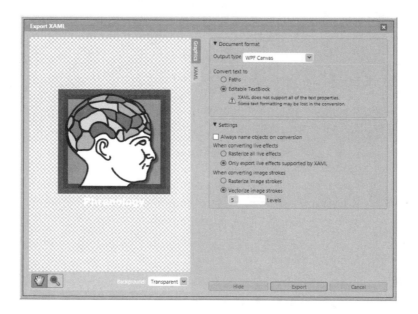

This dialog box features a large preview pane on the left side, which gives an accurate representation of how the target application will render the exported XAML code. (To hide the preview pane, click Hide. To show the preview pane again, click Preview.) As you work through the rest of this exercise, keep your eye on the preview pane.

> **Tip** To adjust the view and magnification level of the preview pane, use the Pan and Zoom tools at the bottom of the dialog box. You can also right-click the preview pane to set the magnification level from the context menu that appears, or you can zoom in and out with the scroll wheel on your mouse.

At any time, you can switch between a visual preview and the actual XAML code by clicking the Graphics and XAML tabs on the right side of the preview pane.

> **Tip** By default, Expression Design exports the blank areas of your artboard as transparent, but you can specify a solid white or solid black background instead by choosing White or Black from the Background menu.

6. On the **Output type** menu, click **Silverlight Canvas**.

You are exporting this file for use in a Silverlight application, so you want to format the XAML code in a way that maximizes Silverlight compatibility. For other applications, choose a different XAML format, such as one of the following:

- **WPF Canvas.** Choose this format for general use in Expression Blend.

- **WPF Resource Dictionary.** Choose this format to create reusable assets for Expression Blend.

- **Silverlight Canvas.** As already mentioned, choose this format for use in a Silverlight application.

> **Tip** The remaining options in the Export XAML dialog box change slightly, depending on your choice of output type.

In the preview pane, notice that many elements seem to be missing: There are no black strokes around the letters, no drop shadow under the head, and no image stroke around the background box. We'll deal with each element in turn.

7. Under **Convert text to**, click **Paths**.

This option guarantees that the text will look exactly as it does in your document window, but in order to make this guarantee, Expression Design must convert the text into paths. If you have already converted your text objects into paths, then this option has no effect on the XAML code.

The alternative option, Editable TextBlock, maintains the editability of the text in the target application, although the look of the text might change, because XAML does not support the complete set of appearance attributes for text objects.

> **Tip** When in doubt, export two copies of the XAML file: one with text converted to paths, and one with editable text. Inspect both in your target application, and if the editable text looks decent enough, go with that version.

8. In the **Settings** section, under **When converting live effects**, click **Rasterize all live effects**.

This option causes the drop shadow to return in the preview pane, although the shadow takes the form of a pixel-based image object. It no longer has the properties of a live effect. The bitmap shadow should look all right as long as you don't change the dimensions of the interface design in the target application. If you do—especially if you scale up—you risk a loss of image quality.

The other option, Only Export Live Effects Supported By XAML, maintains your effects as effects. However, if a live effect is not supported by XAML—such as the drop shadow in the interface design—Expression Design will not export it, and it disappears from the preview pane.

9. Under **When converting image strokes**, click **Rasterize image strokes**.

This option causes Expression Design to convert the image stroke to a bitmap graphic, which ensures that the exported XAML looks exactly like the original.

The other option, Vectorize Image Strokes, causes Expression Design to convert the image stroke into vector graphics, which makes them more transformable in the target application, but it might also alter their appearance. You can improve the level of detail in a vectorized image stroke by increasing the value in the Levels slider, but your degree of success will vary. Some image strokes, such as the one in the illustration on the following page, do not look right unless you rasterize them.

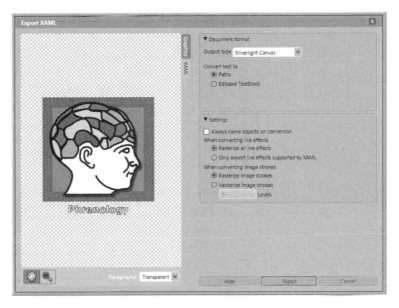

10. Click **Export**.

The Export XAML dialog box closes, and Expression Design saves the XAML file to the designated location on your computer. The file is now ready for service in Silverlight.

Tip When you rasterize elements in your design, Expression Design creates bitmap images for them, These bitmaps appear in a new folder at the same location as the exported XAML file. The folder takes the same name as the XAML file plus the suffix _files. So if the name of the XAML file is *phrenology*, the rasterized elements are put in a folder called *phrenology_files*. This folder is just as important as the XAML file itself, so keep it safe, and if you ever move the XAML file, be sure to move the _files folder to the same location.

CLOSE all open documents without saving any changes.

Exporting Your Art to PDF

You can use Adobe's amazingly successful Portable Document Format—*PDF*—to create an exported version of your document that preserves the vector nature of your vector graphics. All the other export formats (except for XAML) give you pixel-based results, but with PDF, you get paths. Not all Expression Design features translate gracefully to the kinds of paths that PDF supports, so you might need to indulge in a little rasterization, but depending on the simplicity of your design aesthetic, your work might not require any rasterization at all.

PDF does not support some of the appearance attributes in Expression Design, and rasterizing these *usually* makes your exported PDF resemble the original more closely. In the Export PDF dialog box, you have three choices:

- **Transparent gradients.** Select this check box to convert partially transparent gradients into bitmap images. If you leave this check box cleared, Expression Design will export the gradient as closely as possible without rasterization.

    > **Tip** Transparency can be difficult for Expression Design to render in rasterized form for a PDF, so you might have better luck leaving this check box cleared.

- **Image strokes.** Select this check box to convert image strokes into bitmap images. If you leave this check box cleared, Expression Design attempts to vectorize the stroke. Set the level of detail for the vectorization by choosing a value from the Levels menu.

    > **Tip** Some image strokes are too complex to be vectorized, so Expression Design exports them as standard strokes unless you choose to rasterize them.

- **Live effects.** Select this check box to convert all live effects into bitmap images. If you leave this check box cleared, Expression Design will either vectorize or ignore all live effects in use.

    > **Tip** The Resolution setting controls the resolution of any rasterized elements. For best results, set the resolution to match that of the document window.

In this exercise, you will export an Expression Design document to PDF.

USE the *dragon.design* file. This practice file is located in the *Documents\Microsoft Press\ Expression Design SBS\ExportingWork* folder.

OPEN the *dragon.design* file.

1. Look at the illustration, which features a stylized dragon. Again, the use of effects and image strokes exceeds the boundaries of good taste, but this image helps demonstrate how to work with PDF.

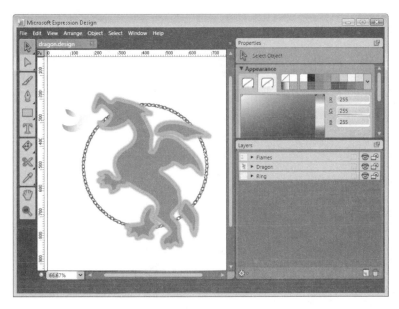

2. On the **File** menu, click **Export**.

   The Export dialog box opens.

3. On the **Save as type** menu, click **PDF (*.pdf)**.

4. Type **dragon_vectorized** in the **File name** field.

   You will create a second version of the exported PDF later in this exercise.

5. Navigate to a convenient location on your computer by using the standard controls in the dialog box.

   Expression Design will save the exported PDF in your chosen location. Your *Pictures* folder is never a bad choice.

6. Click **Save**.

The Export dialog box closes, and the Export PDF dialog box opens.

7. Note that in this dialog box, you can select those design elements that you want to convert to bitmap images in the PDF. For the purposes of this exercise, clear all three rasterization check boxes.

8. Click **OK**.

The Export PDF dialog box closes, and Expression Design saves the PDF file to the specified location.

9. In Windows Explorer, navigate to the location where you saved the PDF, and double-click the file to view it in Adobe Reader.

Tip You probably have Adobe Reader installed on your computer already, but if you don't, you can install it for free from *www.adobe.com/products/acrobat/readstep2.html*.

As you can tell, the transparent gradient fared pretty well, but the outer glow and the image stroke are both gone.

10. Repeat steps 2–9, this time naming the file **dragon_rasterized** and selecting all three rasterization check boxes in step 7. Set the resolution to 96 dpi, which is the same resolution as the document window.

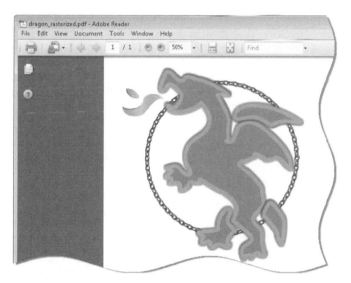

When you have opened this file in Adobe Reader, compare it to the vectorized version.

It would seem that the image stroke and live effects work better as bitmaps, while the transparent gradient looks better un-rasterized, at least for this particular image.

CLOSE all open documents without saving any changes.

Printing Your Art

Printing in Expression Design is very similar to exporting, in that the software rasterizes any vector graphics before sending the data to the printer, and the entire visible contents of the artboard are printed unless you specify a crop region.

> **Tip** To change general print settings, point to Options on the Edit menu, and then click Print And Export.

Because the printer is printing a rasterized file, resolution becomes an important consideration. With Expression Design, you can set the desired resolution before you begin printing.

In this exercise, you will print a piece of vector art.

> **USE** the *knight.design* file. This practice file is located in the *Documents\Microsoft Press\ Expression Design SBS\ExportingWork* folder.
>
> **OPEN** the *knight.design* file.

1. Look at this illustration. It's a graphic design of the knight chess piece, all done with vectors.

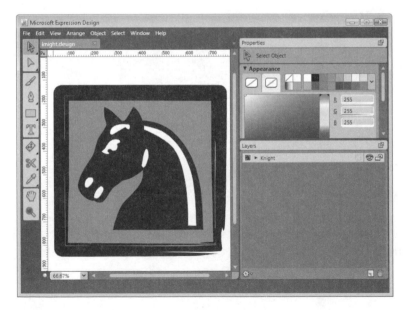

2. On the **File** menu, click **Print**.

The standard Print dialog box opens.

3. On the **Name** menu, click your printer, and then click **Properties**.

A dialog box containing printing options opens.

4. Review the settings for your printer. If necessary, set the paper size and the orientation of the print. If controls for these options are not there, click **Advanced**.

> **Tip** You should also set the printer's resolution to the desired output for the art. Although Expression Design can easily translate the resolution in a later step, your work will look its best if the printer resolution matches the output resolution. Look for your printer's default resolution setting in the advanced print options.

5. After setting the page size and orientation, click **OK**.

The dialog box closes.

6. In the **Print** dialog box, click **OK**.

The Print dialog box closes, and the Print Rasterization Settings dialog box opens. Here is where you determine the resolution of the printed art.

7. On the **dpi** menu, click the desired resolution.

For the best results, use the option labeled (printer setting). This way, Expression Design doesn't have to do as much pixel manipulation.

> **Tip** If the desired resolution is not labeled (Printer Setting) in the Print Rasterization Settings dialog box, you can always cancel the current operation and then repeat these steps, changing the printer resolution setting in the Print Properties dialog box until you get the resolution you're looking for.

8. Select the **Center Page** check box.

This option centers the artwork on the printed page.

9. Click **OK**.

The Print Rasterization Settings dialog box closes, and Expression Design sends your artwork to the printer that you chose in step 3.

> **CLOSE** the *knight.design* file without saving any changes. If you are not continuing directly to the Appendix, exit Expression Design.

Key Points

- By default, all visible elements on the artboard of the document window are included when you export or print. Hidden elements and elements outside the artboard's frame are excluded.

- You can set crop marks on the artboard to define a specific region as the part to export or print.

- You can export your work in various pixel-based formats, such as .tiff, .jpeg, and .bmp, which makes sharing your files more convenient.

- With Expression Design, you can export individual image objects directly from the document window.

- You can export your document as a block of XAML code for use in Expression Blend and other XAML-aware applications. XAML does not support all features of Expression Design, so you might need to rasterize certain effects and other elements to get them to display as you designed them.

- You can also export your document in PDF format, which preserves many of the vector objects in your design as paths. With Expression Design, you can rasterize those elements that PDF does not support, such as live effects.

- Before printing, Expression Design asks you to choose the output resolution of the printed document. For best results, set the output resolution to the default resolution of your printer.

Appendix: Setting Preferences in Expression Design

Users of Microsoft Expression Design need and expect to be able to produce artwork that can be used in many different ways—exported to a raster program, published on the Web, printed, or used in a video, to name a few. This circumstance, along with the preferences and individual needs of the users themselves, means that the same options are not always the best for everyone. Fortunately, Expression Design lets you customize the way it works for the way *you* work.

You do this by adjusting the various settings in the Options dialog box. This Appendix walks you through all of the options available in this dialog box.

To access the Options dialog box, click Options on the Edit menu, or use the Ctrl+K keyboard shortcut. The dialog box opens with its General page active. (To choose one of the other pages, click its name in the menu.)

General Options

General

The following options are available under this heading:

- **Quick (area) select.** Selected by default, this check box lets you click and drag— select and move—in one motion of the mouse. If you clear this check box, you will need to first deliberately select objects by clicking on them before you can change them. Because objects can be moved or edited only if they are first selected, this helps ensure that you will not accidentally move objects.

- **Transform image fill.** By default, when you transform an object that has an image fill, the fill will transform with the object. Clear this check box if you want patterns to remain in their original size and orientation, despite any object transformations.

- **Path operations: Keep originals.** This is cleared by default. If you want to keep the source paths after using path operations, select this check box.

- **Create new layer above current layer.** By default, this check box is selected. When a new layer is created, it is placed above the currently selected layer. Clearing this check box will cause new layers to be inserted at the top of the list in the Layers panel.

- **Automatically commit transforms.** This check box is cleared by default, so that as you make transformations, Expression Design remembers each step but doesn't actually commit the transformation until you tell it to. When you select this check box, the transformations will be committed as they are applied.

Mouse Wheel

The following options are available under this heading:

- **Mouse wheel usage.** By default, the mouse wheel is used for zooming to magnify the page, but you can use the menu here to change the behavior to Vertical Scrolling for scrolling vertically (or horizontally when you hold down the Shift key) or Horizontal Scrolling for scrolling horizontally (or vertically when you hold down the Shift key). When either of these two scrolling options is selected, you can make the mouse wheel zoom by holding down the Ctrl key.

- **Mouse wheel zoom about mouse position.** When the mouse wheel is set up for zooming, this option controls the center of magnification. If you clear this check box, you will always zoom in or out based on the center of the visible page. When this check box is selected, as it is by default, the pointer position is used as the zoom center.

Color Dropper

The following option is available under this heading:

- **Picked color.** By default, the Color Dropper picks up the color that is applied to the object you click, not considering opacity. If you click Screen Color on this menu, the Color Dropper will pick up the RGB equivalent of the color shown on the screen, taking into account the opacity of the color of the object on which you click.

Messages and Warnings

The following option is available under this heading:

- **Display all messages and warnings.** If you want to all messages and warnings to be displayed, select this check box.

Workspace Options

User Interface

The following options are available under this heading:

- **Theme.** In Expression Design, you can choose the theme, or "look," of the interface. The default is Expression Dark, but you can also choose Expression Light from the menu. If you think Expression Light looks familiar, that's because it does. The illustrations in this book use that very theme.

- **Workspace zoom.** You can set the default workspace zoom level with this slider. The default setting for this option is 100 percent.

Stroke Options

Stroke

The following options are available under this heading:

- **Drawing tools append to path.** With this check box selected, you can start or end new paths at existing open paths. Note that this check box applies only to drawing tools that place anchor points, such as the Pen tool, the Line tool, the B-Spline tool, and the Polyline tool. The Paintbrush has its own path-appending controls. This check box has the same effect as the Append To Line check box in the Properties panel when you choose the Line tool and no objects are selected on the page.

- **Scale stroke width.** By default, when you scale a path with a basic or gradient stroke, the width of the stroke does not change. Select this check box to make the stroke width scale with the object. Note: This does not affect brush strokes.

Freehand Tool

The following options are available under this heading:

- **Show pressure trail.** When you draw with the Paintbrush tool, Expression Design displays the actual size of the stroke by default. If you clear this check box, only a thin line will show as you draw, and the final shape and size will display only after the path is complete. *Pressure trail* is a term that refers to the fact that you can change the width of a line by pressing harder with the stylus when using a drawing tablet.

- **Tightness of fit.** When you draw with the Paintbrush tool, Expression Design smoothes the path as you go, to compensate for slightly shaky hands. This option lets you make a selection from the menu to choose how much smoothing is applied. The tighter a curve is fitted, the closer the final path will be to the shape you drew, and the more anchor points the curve will have. The default setting is Normal.

- **Enable pressure sensitivity.** This check box is selected by default. If you have a pressure-sensitive graphics tablet such as a Wacom, use this feature to enable pressure sensitivity when using the Paintbrush tool. If you are not using a tablet and stylus, this setting has no effect.

- **Pressure scale.** Pressure scale is set to 1.20 by default, which means that when you apply maximum pressure with the stylus, the stroke width will be 10 x 1.2 pixels, or 12 pixels. Settings can range from 1.0 to 2.0.

Z-Axis Rotation

The following options are available under this heading:

- **Pan tool rotates paper.** This check box is selected by default. Use it if you want the Pan tool to rotate the paper using the tilt or 4D setting of your tablet stylus or mouse. If your tablet or mouse doesn't offer this feature, selecting this check box does nothing.

- **Direct object rotation.** This check box is selected by default. When it is selected, you can rotate your 4D mouse or tilt your tablet stylus to rotate selected objects when any of the selection tools are chosen from the Toolbox. This check box is ignored if you don't have a tablet or mouse with this capability.

- **Use pen tilt for rotation.** If you have a tablet capable of reading the tilt angle of the stylus, you can select this check box to have Expression Design use that tilt information to rotate the paper or rotate selected objects.

Display Options

The following options are available under the Display Options heading:

- **Show selected object points.** When this check box is selected, the anchor points on the paths are visible when an object is selected. Clearing this check box hides the anchor points. This is selected by default.

- **Show resize handles.** When this check box is selected, selected objects display the resize handles around the selection. Clearing this check box hides the resize handles. This is selected by default.

- **Display transparency.** You can clear this check box if you want all objects to display with 100 percent opacity and not show the transparency that is applied to them. This is useful to show how the image would display when exported to an image format that doesn't support transparency. Display Transparency is on by default.

- **Greek limit.** When text is greeked in Expression Design, it shows up as a gray bar on the screen rather than as individual characters. If your artwork contains very small text, Expression Design might be slow to display your image, so you can set this slider to show text smaller than a certain size as greeked text, speeding up the display and screen redraw. The default setting is 10, which means that all text smaller than 10 pixels will be greeked. Use the slider to adjust the setting from 1 to 100 pixels. Greeking text on screen does not affect the output, only your on-screen view.

- **Show printable area.** When this check box is selected, an outline of the default printer's default page size is shown, with the printable area outlined on the page. Because your document frame might be a different size, this can give you an idea of how your image will look on the final printed page. It has no effect on how the page prints. This check box is cleared by default.

Unit and Grid Options

Units

The controls in the Units section let you choose the units of measurement for documents, strokes, and type; you can set these in inches, millimeters, centimeters, picas, points, or pixels. Choose the one that works best with your output. For example, if you are printing an image, you might choose inches so that you can view your image in its final print size; if you are working on an image for the Web, pixels would be a better choice.

The following options are available under the Units heading:

- **Document units.** The default setting for Document Units is pixels. You can use the menu to change to any of the other units. The measurement you choose is shown in the page rulers, on the Action Bar, and anywhere else that a unit of measurement is specified.

- **Stroke units.** The default unit of measurement for stroke width is pixels, but you can use this menu to change to any of the other units. This affects the Stroke Width slider in the Appearance category of the Properties panel.

- **Type units.** The default Type Units setting is points, which is common to page layout programs and so is a logical choice in Expression Design. Expression Design uses the units selected here when you specify type size and baseline offset.

Grids and Guides

The following option is available under this heading:

- **Grid size.** The grid size is the distance between the lines on the grid. The default setting is 32 pixels. If you change the Document Units setting, the grid size will change accordingly. Use the slider to increase or decrease the grid spacing.

Rulers

The following option is available under this heading:

- **Ruler origin is always top left of artboard.** By default, this setting is selected so that the ruler origin, where x and y both equal 0, will be at the upper-left corner of the artboard. Clearing this check box displays the 0,0 point in the lower-left corner of the document page whenever the document units are set to anything other than pixels. When the document units are set to pixels, the 0,0 point will always be at the upper-left corner. You can override the default position of the 0,0 point by clicking Set Document Origin on the File menu and then clicking anywhere inside the document frame to place a custom 0,0 point.

Arrangement

The following options are available under this heading:

- **Rotation Steps.** When you hold the Shift key as you rotate an object by dragging its transform handles, you constrain the rotation angle based on the value set in this slider. The default for this option is 8, which means that when you press the Shift key you constrain the rotation to 45-degree angles. This is figured by dividing 360 degrees by the angle to which you want to constrain the rotation; for example, 360 degrees divided by 45 equals 8 steps.

- **Nudge Increment.** The Nudge Increment slider controls how far the selected anchor point or object moves when an Arrow key is pressed. The setting is in the same unit of measurement as the document unit, and is set at 1 px by default (because pixels are the default document unit.) You can choose any value, starting with 0 (at which pressing an Arrow key doesn't move the selection at all). You can go as high as 416.67 when the document unit is pixels, although this changes if the document unit changes. For example, if the document unit is set to points, you can choose between 0 and 100 points for the nudge increment.

  When you are nudging, you can hold the Ctrl key as you press an Arrow key to nudge the selection by 1/10 of the nudge increment value, or hold the Shift key as you press an Arrow key to nudge the selection by 10 times the nudge increment value.

- **Stack gap size.** The Stack feature places objects 10 pixels away from each other by default. You can use this slider to change the value anywhere between -2666.67 and 2666.67 pixels. Values between -2000 and 2000 can be chosen if the document unit is points.

File Options

Native Format Save Options

The following option is available under this heading:

- **Autosave frequency.** You can choose how often Expression Design saves your open files for backup and recovery. The default is Normal, but you can choose from Never, Seldom (about every 5 minutes), Normal (about every 30 seconds), or Frequent (every 5 seconds).

Document Thumbnails

The following options are available under this heading:

- **Thumbnail size.** By default, Expression Design files are saved with a large thumbnail that is displayed when you use the Open dialog box. You can change this by choosing Off, Small, or Large from this menu.
- **Thumbnail image range.** This setting determines which objects display in the thumbnail image. You can click Page Frame in this menu to display only what shows within the page frame boundaries, click Crop Marks to display only objects within crop marks (if you have any set up), or click Objects Bounding Box to display all objects on the document even if they are outside the artboard boundaries.

Import

The following options are available under this heading:

- **Create import summaries.** When you have the Create Import Summaries check box selected, Expression Design displays a summary of any errors it encounters because of non-supported features when you are importing images that were created in an earlier version of Expression or Expression Design. Clear the check box to hide the summary. This is selected by default.
- **Show import warning dialog box.** Selected by default, this check box tells Expression Design to display an alert dialog box whenever you open documents that were created in earlier versions of Expression or Expression Design.

Clipboard (XAML) Options

The settings in this dialog box duplicate those in the XAML Export dialog box. If the Document Format or Effects section is closed, you can expand it by clicking the arrow next to the heading.

Document Format

The following options are available under this heading:

- **Canvas.** To create objects that can be animated or manipulated interactively, as you would need to do to use them in Microsoft Expression Blend, select the Canvas method. Then select one of the following options:
  - **Export editable TextBlocks.** Turned on by default, this option maintains text as individual editable characters.
  - **Export flattened paths.** Turned off by default, this option maintains the look of the text by converting each character to outlines. The text is no longer editable, but it is more likely to maintain the appearance of the original text.

- **Silverlight.** To create a file that will be suitable for display in an application built for Microsoft Silverlight, choose the Silverlight option.

- **Resource dictionary.** To treat the content as a collection of reusable assets, you can select the Resource Dictionary method. Here you choose from three methods of grouping:

  - **Document** generates a single resource for the entire document.

  - **Layers** generates a resource for each layer in the document.

  - **Objects** generates a resource for each object in the document.

  You can also select from two types of output for paths:

  - **Drawing brush** creates resources that can be used inside XAML wherever a Brush type can be used.

  - **Drawing image** creates resources that must be wrapped inside a Brush but are faster to render.

Effects

If the list is collapsed, click the arrow to expand it. The following options are available under this heading:

- **Rasterize live effects.** This check box is cleared by default. When it is selected, Expression Design can rasterize live effects, turning them into bitmapped images. This helps maintain the appearance of your artwork as much as possible. If you clear this check box, some objects might be exported as solid lines or fills.

- **Vectorize image strokes.** Selected by default, this check box tells Expression Design to vectorize image brush strokes into overlapping solid fill objects for the export. Use the slider to choose one of five levels. Small vectorization levels will simplify the exported image stroke. Larger vectorization levels add more detail to the exported image stroke.

Print and Export Options

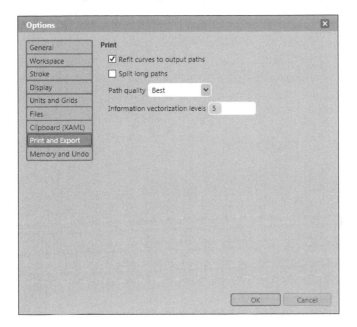

These options affect how images are exported from Expression Design, whether you are printing, saving, or copying to the Clipboard.

Print

The following options are available under this heading:

- **Refit curves to output paths.** Curves created in Expression Design are defined by B-Spline and other mathematical curves that are difficult to translate into ordinary PostScript Bézier curves. When you print or export vector artwork, Expression Design attempts to recreate these paths as closely as possible, resulting in dozens or hundreds of anchor points per object. This check box is selected by default, letting Expression Design map strokes and paths inexactly. The result is usually similar in appearance, but with far fewer anchor points, making it easier to print or work with in another application.

- **Split long paths.** Extremely long or complex paths can cause trouble when you are printing, especially if you have an older laser printer. Selecting this check box lets Expression Design split complex paths into simpler paths. The result should be visually identical.

- **Path quality.** By default, Expression Design is set to Best when exporting or printing. You can choose Draft or Normal from the menu for lower quality.

- **Information vectorization levels.** The default setting for the number of levels used to vectorize image strokes in file exports is 5, but you can use the slider to select any value from 1 to 16 levels, 1 being the least accurate and 16 being the most accurate (as well as having the most anchor points). This is a process similar to using the Auto Trace Image feature when working with bitmap images.

Memory and Undo Options

Memory

The following options are available under this heading:

- **Frozen layer memory limit.** Freezing a layer turns a layer's objects to a bitmap at a resolution of your choice by rasterizing. At high resolutions, freezing can be memory intensive and affect program performance. This option lets you specify an upper limit to the amount of memory Expression Design can use for rasterizing each layer. The default setting is 128 MB (megabytes).

- **Undo levels (after restart).** With this option, you can set the number of undo levels between 2 and 200. The default is 40. You must exit Expression Design and restart the program for this change to take effect.

Glossary

Action Bar A horizontal pane across the bottom of the program window that changes dynamically to display information pertinent to the selected object or objects, such as position on the page and size. The Action Bar can also be used to manipulate objects with precise control. You hide or show the pane by clicking Action Bar on the Window menu.

align To make two or more objects parallel using the same point on each. You can align objects to top edges, bottom edges, right or left edges, or vertical or horizontal centers.

alpha transparency An alpha stop in a gradient fill defines the amount of transparency at the point of the stop on the gradient bar.

anchor point A point on a vector path, also known as a *node*. Anchor points can be moved to manipulate a path.

anti-aliasing A technique for creating the appearance of smooth edges in a bitmap graphic by blending the colors of the pixels on the edge of a figure with the colors of the background pixels.

area text Text that displays inside a path.

artboard A document frame in the work area in the shape of a page. Anything placed on the artboard is printable and exportable. Likewise, if a live effect is applied to an object that is only partially on the artboard, the effect will show only on the area that is on the artboard.

attribute A characteristic of an object, such as fill color or opacity, stroke color or opacity, or brush stroke.

auto tracing The automatic process of converting a raster graphic to a vector graphic.

Back Minus Front A path operation in which the shape of the front object is removed from the shape of the back object. The resulting object retains the attributes of the original back object.

baseline In a text object, the line upon which the glyphs fall. Some glyphs, such as the lowercase p, have descenders that dip below the baseline.

baseline offset In a text object, the amount by which a glyph is placed above or below the baseline.

Bézier curve A form of Bézier path; a path defined by a mathematical formula rather than pixels. Displayed on the page as a series of anchor points and line segments, a Bézier path can be straight or curved. Also known as *Bézier paths*.

bitmap An image defined by small squares of color called *pixels*. A photo is an example of a bitmap image. Also called a *raster image*.

Blend Mode A setting that determines how an object's colors interact with the colors of objects below.

Blend Paths A command that blends a series of interim objects, called *in-betweens*, between two or more selected paths, taking into consideration the position and attributes of the objects as well as the number of steps and method of interpolation.

B-Spline curve A vector path created with the B-Spline tool. A B-Spline path is defined by a series of points that indicate the direction the path should follow. Anchor points on a B-Spline path can be curve or corner control points. Though similar to a Bézier path, a B-Spline curve is described by anchor points placed off the actual path.

B-Spline tool The tool used to create B-Spline curves. It is found in the Pen tool group in the Toolbox.

brush stroke A vector or bitmap image placed along a vector path. The stroke conforms to the path and updates when the path is edited. Also known as a *skeletal stroke*.

buttons Controls on the panels, such as the More Buttons, that show advanced properties. These buttons allow options to be hidden until needed to provide more room in the pane for the panels.

clipping mask An object placed over or under another to hide the area of the second object that is outside the mask. For example, you could place a circle on top of a photo, select the photo and the circle, and make a clipping mask from the circle. All that would be visible would be the area of the photo that falls inside the circle. In previous versions of the program, this was known as a *clipper*. Also known as a *clipping path*.

clipping mask group The objects contained in a clipping mask.

clipping path *See* clipping mask.

clone A duplicate of a path that can have different fill and stroke attributes, but that will be changed when the shape of the original (called the *master*) changes. *See also* duplicate.

closed path A path that has the same start and end points; a closed shape. A closed path can be a freehand shape or one created with a shape tool, such as a circle.

CMYK Also known as the *four-color model* or *process-color model*, CMYK is a subtractive color model based on four colors: cyan, magenta, yellow, and black. Subtractive color models start with white light. The more color is added, the closer to black the color becomes. Measured in percentages, each color has a value which can range from 0 percent to 100 percent saturation. Usually used on images destined for professional printing.

collide To unintentionally occupy the same space, as in two glyphs that are in the same spot. Increasing the tracking between the glyphs corrects this problem.

Color Picker A control at the top of the Properties panel that is used to choose colors for fills and strokes, colors for gradients, and image fills.

color stop *See* gradient node.

compound path A path made up of two or more sub-paths, each with its own starting and ending anchor points. The inner path will appear to be "cut out" of the outer path. An example of this is a donut shape where the inner path creates a "hole" which is transparent.

compression The method of compacting a computer file so that it requires less storage space.

content Anything on a layer: vector objects, bitmap images, or text.

context menu A menu displayed when you right-click an object or control. The contents change according to what is clicked on the page or interface. The context menu for an object shows actions that can be performed, and the context menu on a control shows additional options.

context-sensitive Dynamic and changing according to the current selection. A menu or panel can be said to be context sensitive.

control handle A handle that extends from a curve or cusp anchor point and that is used to alter the curve, both by moving it to change the angle and thus the direction of the curve, and by changing its length to change the depth of the curve. The longer the handle is, the deeper the curve will be. Also known as a *handle*.

Convert Anchor Point tool A tool found in the Pen tool group in the Toolbox that converts curve anchor points to corner anchor points and vice versa.

cusp point A special anchor point that has two control handles that can be manipulated independently of each other. Cusp anchor points make inner corners possible, and let you adjust the curves for each side of a corner individually.

delete To remove from the page, by pressing either the Delete key or the Backspace key.

descender The portion of a glyph that extends below the baseline.

deselect To make a selected anchor point or object no longer selected. One way to do this is to click a blank area of the document window.

Display Quality A setting that defines how a drawing is shown on the screen: Preview shows the drawing with stroke and fill attributes and is a good indication of how the final output will look. Wireframe shows only a wireframe outline.

distribute To arrange the placement of two or more objects equally in a given space by their tops, bottoms, or centers.

divide A path operation in which the selected paths are cut apart based on where they intersect; all the pieces are retained as separate objects. *See also* intersect.

dock *See* pin.

document A file in Expression Design. The document is where drawing takes place.

document frame The page-shaped area in the document window. Anything in this area will print or export; anything outside the frame will not. *See also* artboard.

document window The workspace in Expression Design. Each open document is contained in a separate document window. The document title is displayed in the flip bar.

drag a marquee To click and drag a square around objects on the page with the Selection tool to select them. All anchor points do not have to be included in the drag; it is enough that the pointer touches the object to include the entire object in the selection.

duplicate An exact copy of an object or group of objects. Each duplicate can be manipulated independently of the others. *See also* clone.

Ellipse tool A shape tool used to draw circles and ellipses. The Ellipse tool is found in the Rectangle tool group in the Toolbox.

encircling To drag an irregular closed shape around an object or objects to select anchor points for editing.

endpoint The last point on an open or closed path.

Fill Rule Rules for how the fill is applied to the overlapping areas when filling a compound path.

Fill tab The tab on the Color Picker that is used to define the attributes of an object's fill.

flip bar A bar across the top of the work area that contains tabs, one for each open document. The flip bar is used to navigate between open documents.

float To unpin or undock, as for a panel. When you click the Float button on a panel you can unpin it from the pane and move it anywhere on the work area. To move a floating panel, drag it by its title bar.

font decoration The type style of a glyph in a text object. Two common font decorations are boldface and italic.

font family The typeface of a glyph in a text object, such as Arial or Times New Roman.

Front Minus Back A path operation in which the shape of the back object is removed from the shape of the front object. The resulting object retains the attributes of the original front object.

glyph A typographical character in a text object that is editable as text.

gradient node A marker on the gradient bar that is used to change the color, transparency, or speed of a gradient. Also called a *color stop* or *gradient stop*.

graphics tablet An input device that lets you draw on a tablet with a pressure-sensitive stylus, often called a *pen*. What is drawn on the tablet's drawing area displays on the screen. With a graphics tablet, you can draw by hand, using greater artistic freedom that the traditional input devices afford. When you use a graphic tablet with a paint program such as Corel Painter, even the thickness of the digital paint and the angle of the stroke can be controlled by stylus tilt and pressure.

grid A non-printable grid that divides the page and is used as an aid in placing objects on the page. You can make the grid visible or invisible on the screen by choosing to show or hide it on the View menu. Objects can be made to snap to the grid for precise control.

group To select and designate objects so that they will be treated as one object for the purposes of scaling, manipulation, and even changing attributes. Objects are grouped by using the commands on the Arrange menu.

handle *See* control handle.

hex A short term for hexadecimal, a base 16 system which uses the numerals from 0 to 9 and the letters from A to F. Each hexadecimal color is made up of three pairs of numbers preceded by a pound sign. The first pair of numbers represent the intensity of red light, the second pair represent the intensity of green light, and the third the intensity of blue light. Red is #FF0000. Broken down it means 100 percent red, 0 percent green, and 0 percent blue. These three pairs of numbers can be combined into millions of colors.

HLS A color model based on hue, lightness, and saturation. Hue is the color and is represented in values ranging from 0 degrees (red) and proceeds through orange, yellow, green, blue, and purple and back to red at 359 degrees. Saturation is the intensity of color and is measured in percentage, from 0 percent (no saturation) to 100 percent (fully saturated, the full value of the color). Lightness is also measured in percentages; 0 percent is the darkest, and 100 percent is lightest.

horizontal alignment The position of the lines of text in a text object. Text lines can be left aligned, right aligned, center aligned, or justified.

horizontal scale The relative width of a glyph in a text object.

HSB A color model based on hue, saturation, and brightness. Hue is the color and is represented in values ranging from 0 degrees (red) and proceeds through orange, yellow, green, blue, and purple and back to red at 359 degrees. Saturation is the intensity of color and is measured in percentage, from 0 percent (no saturation) to 100 percent (fully saturated, the full value of the color). Brightness is also measured in percentages; 0 percent is the darkest, and 100 percent is lightest.

image object An image whose dimensions are defined by pixels rather than vectors.

in-between An object in between the original paths of a path blend. *See* Blend Path.

intersect A path operation in which selected paths are cut apart based on where they intersect. Only the pieces that intersect are retained; the rest are discarded. The attributes of the top path are applied to the remaining shapes. *See also* divide.

layer A transparent virtual page on which an object or objects are placed in a drawing. Objects placed on the layer hide the objects that are on the layers below them.

Layers panel The Expression Design interface panel that lets you manipulate layers, hiding and showing them, changing their stacking order, and locking or unlocking them. This panel is pinned to the pane, but you can float it in the workspace if desired.

leading The amount of space between lines of type in a text object.

Line tool A shape tool used to draw straight lines. The Line tool is under the Rectangle tool group in the Toolbox.

live effect A bitmap effect applied non-destructively to objects on the page. Live effects remain editable and fully reversible until the document is exported.

locked A layer that is secured so that it cannot be edited. Locking a layer protects it from accidental changes. *See also* unlocked layer.

lossless A type of compression in which the information in an image file is organized more efficiently without the loss of any data.

lossy A type of compression in which the information in an image file is organized more efficiently along with the loss of some extraneous data. The higher the degree of lossy compression, the more likely that image quality will noticeably degrade.

mask A path used to hide parts of the object below. For example, you could use an ellipse to create a mask on a photo, hiding everything outside the elliptical masked area.

midpoint slider The midpoint marker on the gradient bar that marks the halfway point of the transition of color or transparency. Move the slider to change the midpoint.

node *See* anchor point; gradient node.

nudge To move an object in small, precise increments by pressing the Arrow keys on the keyboard.

object A path, either closed or open. A drawing can be composed of hundreds of individual objects. For example, in a drawing of a tree, each leaf would be one object.

opacity The transparency of a fill or stroke, measured in percentage. At 100 percent opacity, an object is completely opaque; at 0 percent opacity, the object is completely transparent. All percentages in between render degrees of transparency.

open path A path that has a start point and endpoint that are not joined. Lines and arcs are examples of open paths.

Page Another word for the document artboard area.

pane An area of the application window reserved for panels, such as the Layers panel or the Properties panel.

path A vector line or object defined by a series of anchor points and segments.

Path view A display view that shows only the outline of the original path, not the shape of brush strokes. This display view is available only on the Layers panel in the Options menu under Layer Options. The Layer Render Style command for this view is applied on a layer-by-layer basis and therefore cannot be applied to individual objects. Render Styles chosen in the Layers panel take precedence over Display Quality chosen in the View menu.

PDF (Portable Document Format) A file format that maintains the presentation of a document across multiple devices and platforms. When Expression Design exports artwork in this format, vector objects are not necessarily converted to bitmaps.

pin To attach a panel to the pane on the right side of the workspace. Also called *dock*.

pixel The smallest unit of area on a bitmap image. Pixel is short for *picture element*.

pixilated Displayed at such a large size that the image becomes fuzzy and the individual pixels are visible. Pixilated applies to bitmap images.

Polygon tool A shape tool used to draw multi-sided objects other than squares or rectangles, such as triangles, octagons, and stars. The Polygon tool is under the Rectangle tool group in the Toolbox.

Polyline tool A Bézier path tool that lets you add straight or curved segments as you draw. The Polyline tool is used with the modifier keys. This tool is under the Pen tool group in the Toolbox.

Preview The display view that shows the drawing with colors, fills, and strokes visible.

Properties panel The panel used to set the properties of objects, determining their color, stroke, and opacity. The Properties panel is pinned to the pane, but you can float it in the workspace if desired.

raster image An image composed of pixels rather than vector mathematical formulas. A photo is an example of a raster image. Raster image formats include .bmp, .jpeg, and .tiff. Also referred to as a *bitmap image*.

raster program An application whose primary function is the editing and creation of raster, or bitmap, images.

rasterize To convert a vector image into a bitmap image format. Rasterizing removes the vector editing capabilities from the image.

Rectangle tool A shape tool used to draw squares or rectangles. The Rectangle tool is by default at the top of the Rectangle Tool group in the Toolbox.

redo To reverse the last Undo action.

reference point The point on an object from which transformations originate. For example, if you select the bottom-left reference point in the Registration button on the Action Bar when preparing to rotate an image, the image will rotate around the bottom-left corner of the object.

Registration button The button in the Action Bar that is used to set the reference point of an object.

reverse a path To swap the start point and endpoint of a path, which reverses the path's direction and the flow of the stroke along the path.

revert To go back to a former state; reverting returns a document to the state at which it was last saved.

RGB An additive color model used in monitor screens and home printing. RGB color model combines three colors (also called *channels*), Red, Green, and Blue, to make millions of colors on screen. Every pixel in an image is assigned an intensity value from 0 to 255 for the red (R), green (G), and blue (B) values. The three colors together at their strongest intensity (R255, G255, B255) is white. R0, G0, B0 is black. Any other value equal for all three channels is gray; the higher the number, the darker the gray.

scale To increase or decrease the dimensions of an object.

Scissors tool The tool used to split an open path into two or more paths, or to convert a closed path to an open one by breaking the path.

script The property of a glyph in a text object that determines whether Expression Design displays the glyph as a subscript, a superscript, or a regular character.

scroll bar A sliding bar on a window or panel that is used to display the content that does not fit into the current view. Drag the bar to scroll and display the rest of the window's or panel's contents. Scroll bars are among the controls known as *widgets*.

segment The portion of a path between anchor points.

select To make an object or objects active. Objects cannot be edited unless they are selected.

selection An active object or objects.

simplify To remove extraneous anchor points from a path to create a smoother path.

skeletal stroke Another name for a brush stroke.

skew To tilt an object on one of its axes; also called *shearing*.

slider A control on a panel or on the Action Bar that lets you "scrub" the pointer over the data area to change the properties. Sliders are among the controls known as *widgets*.

speed (gradient) The rate at which one color blends into another in a gradient.

split a path To divide a path with the Scissors tool into two or more paths, which then become independent objects. A closed path becomes an open path once it has been split.

stacking order The order in which objects display on the page; the object highest in the stacking order is in front of the other objects, and the object lowest in the stacking order is behind the other objects.

start point The first anchor point on an open or closed path.

Stop Alpha slider (gradient) A control used to add transparency to a gradient.

Stroke Definition box The control used to define a custom stroke.

Stroke tab The tab on the Color Picker that is used to define the attributes of a stroke.

subscript A glyph smaller than its surrounding characters that is placed below the baseline in a text object.

superscript A glyph smaller than its surrounding characters that is placed above the baseline in a text object.

text object A special kind of vector graphic that contains glyphs, or typographical characters that are editable as text.

tool group A group of similar tools in the Toolbox that are displayed on a menu when the active tool in the tool group is clicked.

Toolbox A panel containing the Expression Design tools. The Toolbox normally sits along the left side of the work area, but you can hide it with an option on the Window menu.

tracing To convert a raster image to a vector image. The tracing process is often called *auto tracing* when the software application completes it automatically.

tracking The amount of space between two or more glyphs in a text object.

type size The standard height or overall dimensions of a glyph in a text object.

undo To reverse the last change to a file.

ungroup To return a group of objects to individual object status so they can no longer be edited as a group.

unite A path operation in which the selected paths are joined to create a single object. The new object retains the fill and stroke attributes of the front object.

unlocked A layer that is fully editable. *See also* locked layer.

vector graphic An image created by using vector drawing tools, composed of anchor points and segments as opposed to pixels. Also known as a *vector illustration*.

vector program An application whose primary function is to create vector illustrations.

widget A term that collectively describes the buttons, sliders, and scroll bar controls on a panel.

Wireframe A display view that shows the drawing as path and stroke outlines.

workspace The area on the program window in which document windows reside and all editing takes place.

XAML (Extensible Application Markup Language) A computer language used to describe graphical displays and user interfaces.

Index

O

P

About the Authors

Sara Froehlich

Sara Froehlich is a contributing writer for *Photoshop Elements Techniques*. She is an instructor at Eclectic Academy at *www.eclecticacademy.com* and LVS Online at *www.lvsonline.com,* where she teaches classes on Adobe Illustrator, Photoshop Elements, and other graphics programs. She is the Photoshop instructor at Digital Art Academy at *www.digitalartacademy.com.*

Over the past five years, she has authored 35 six-week courses in Adobe Photoshop and Photoshop Elements, Adobe Illustrator, Adobe Acrobat, Xara Xtreme, Corel PHOTO-PAINT, Macromedia Dreamweaver, Macromedia Freehand, and Macromedia Fireworks, among others. She also co-authored a Creature House Expression 3 course with Annie Ford. Her Web site, *www.northlite.net,* has more information on her classes, as well as tutorials for Microsoft Expression Design, Adobe Illustrator, and Adobe Photoshop.

Thanks

Many thanks to Sandra Haynes, Rosemary Caperton, Susie Bayers, Juliana Aldous, Nancy Muir, and the whole Microsoft Press crew. Very many thanks to Marc Campbell.

Undying gratitude goes to Tom, my partner and husband of 33 years, for doing everything in his power to let me have writing time. I truly could not have done this without your love and support, and that of our children.

Marc Campbell

Marc Campbell is a technology author, Web designer, and instructor. His popular guides to computer graphics have appeared around the world in eight languages. Among his professional design credentials are the official sites for DC Comics and *MAD* Magazine and service portals for various state governments.

What do you think of this book?

We want to hear from you!

Do you have a few minutes to participate in a brief online survey?

Microsoft is interested in hearing your feedback so we can continually improve our books and learning resources for you.

To participate in our survey, please visit:

www.microsoft.com/learning/booksurvey/

...and enter this book's ISBN-10 or ISBN-13 number (located above barcode on back cover*). As a thank-you to survey participants in the United States and Canada, each month we'll randomly select five respondents to win one of five $100 gift certificates from a leading online merchant. At the conclusion of the survey, you can enter the drawing by providing your e-mail address, which will be used for prize notification only.

Thanks in advance for your input. Your opinion counts!

*Where to find the ISBN on back cover

ISBN-13: 000-0-0000-0000-0
ISBN-10: 0-0000-0000-0

Example only. Each book has unique ISBN.

Microsoft®
Press

No purchase necessary. Void where prohibited. Open only to residents of the 50 United States (includes District of Columbia) and Canada (void in Quebec). For official rules and entry dates see:

www.microsoft.com/learning/booksurvey/